M000202417

The Imperfect Mom

CANDID CONFESSIONS OF MOTHERS

Edited by Therese J. Borchard

BROADWAY BOOKS

The Imperfect Mom

LIVING IN THE REAL WORLD

NEW YORK

Broadway Books titles may be purchased for business or promotional use or for special sales. For information, please write to: Special Markets Department, Random House, Inc., 1745 Broadway, New York, NY 10019.

PRINTED IN THE UNITED STATES OF AMERICA

BROADWAY BOOKS and its logo, a letter B bisected on the diagonal, are trademarks of Random House, Inc.

Pages 213–15 constitute an extension of this copyright page.

Visit our Web site at www.broadwaybooks.com

Book design by Fritz Metsch

Library of Congress Cataloging-in-Publication Data
The imperfect mom : candid confessions of mothers living in the real world / edited by Therese J. Borchard.
p.   cm.
1. Motherhood. 2. Mothers—Anecdotes. 3. Perfectionism (Personality trait) I. Borchard, Therese Johnson.
HQ759.I46 2006
306.874'3—dc22
2005054342

ISBN-13: 978-0-7679-2266-1
ISBN-10: 0-7679-2266-2

10 9 8 7 6 5 4 3 2 1

First Edition

For Chris LaPanta, my angel with six-pack abs,
who saved little Will.

And for Stacey Hopkins, Will's mom,
who befriended me instead of killing me.

ACKNOWLEDGMENTS

The idea for this book would have never made it safely to my brain had it not been for the suggestion of Suzette Guiffre at *Chesapeake Family* magazine to write an article called "Confessions of an Imperfect Mom," following the harrowing afternoon that the toddler (little Will) under my care was rescued from the fifteen-feet-deep, frigid waters at the city dock in Annapolis, Maryland. Although I was initially peeved at her gall to attach such a label to me, I realized that such a story might relieve the unnecessary burden carried by other closet perfectionist moms.

Of course I thank my new hero, Chris LaPanta, who had the misfortune of choosing my crime scene as the perfect place to chow down some sushi following an Ash Wednesday service where he apparently earned his wings as my angel. Bouquets of roses have gone and still go to Stacey Hopkins, Will's mom, who never once judged me, but instead befriended me and showed me the way a truly kind person would handle that situation.

Hugs and kisses also to my editor, Patricia Medved, who admitted in our first conversation that she was a member of the imperfect club, and who has guided the manuscript with the skill and expertise of a woman who has mastered a trade; to her assistant, Beth Datlowe, who is any writer's dream to work with; and to my best friends at Doubleday, Trace Murphy and Michelle Rapkin, whose insight was invaluable when I held a mere seedling of an idea.

Lots of gratitude go to Claudia Cross, my agent, whose enthusiasm for this project inspired me to go for it, and whose feedback shaped the book into an important contribution to mommy lit.

Boxes of chocolate (they're coming) to Shana Aborn, the first mom I contacted, who e-mailed her list of writer and editor friends, many of which are on the contents page; to Katharine Weber, for her contacts; and to those very brave souls who submitted pieces for the proposal before I could promise a fair compensation: Andrea Buchanan, Deborah Caldwell, Gabrielle Erickson, Muffy Mead-Ferro, Katherine Lee, Jacquelyn Mitchard, Ronnie Polaneczky, Teme Ring, Rochelle Shapiro, Helene Stapinski, Mary Elizabeth Williams, and Caroline Leavitt* (who gets a star next to her name for sharing with me every trick she knows about selling a book).

Mike Leach, my partner on other books, gets credit for everything I write and compile because without his help and mentorship, I wouldn't be writing for the big guys like Broadway; my good friend John Thomas threw out the subtitle that stuck; and Lisa Biedenbach pitched in her two cents at that nice, quiet dinner (the only one that year), where it all came together for the first time.

I know I must be skipping a gazillion people, like all the production, marketing, and publicity staff at Broadway. (Sorry! Although I'm not standing behind a microphone holding an

Oscar, the pressure of an impending deadline has the same effect.)

Last but not least, thank you, Mom, for being a good imperfect mom; thank you, Eric, for loving me despite my imperfections; and thank you, Katherine and David, for providing me with so many opportunities to be imperfect.

Oh! And thanks, Will, for knowing instinctively how to doggy paddle before the lessons. Phew!

CONTENTS

THE PERFECT ENOUGH MOTHER

Kathryn Black

〜〜〜〜〜〜〜〜〜〜〜〜〜〜〜〜〜〜〜〜〜〜〜

My friend laughed, that slightly hysterical oh-my-God laugh, when I told her my dismaying story. In rounding up a gaggle of children from our elementary school to escort them home, I'd forgotten a neighbor's child. I was laughing at seeing myself as recipient of the "Bad Mother of the Month" award, able to laugh because it turned out fine. The girl was a fourth-grader and snagged a ride with someone else. Her mother and I had been trading care of our children for a good decade by then, and she'd let me off easy.

"No worries," my laughing friend told me, "You're a good enough mother."

The label stopped me short. I know it has soothed many an overworked, harried, well-meaning mother; in other words, most of us. Over the decades, though, the "good enough mother" has suffered what a marketing expert might call "image creep." A Google of "good enough" turns up uses like these: "second best, but good enough" and "good enough for government work." These connotations are useful if we're discussing any number of duties that simply aren't worth full-out effort, such as tidying up for company or tackling post-vacation e-mail. But mothering? Second best isn't what most of us had in mind for ourselves or our children.

I'd been mulling this concept over for a while, when in yoga class one day my teacher suggested we each try for a perfect pose. She's not a yogi who pushes and demands. She surely knew that none of us could achieve, on this day, perfection of any kind. But still she said, "Try." As we moved into a cobra pose, she instructed us, "Relax into it. Lead with your heart." That day, I held my cobra a fraction longer, a trifle higher, and much more joyfully. And I thought about mothering.

I decided that, like yoga, it's not whether the outcome is perfect, but whether we've led with our hearts. That's what matters to children. Like every mother I know, I get caught up in that how-much-is-enough/never-enough thinking. Because, in truth, we can never *do* enough. But we can *be* enough for our children.

What if instead of seeing our mothering as "good enough," we thought of ourselves as "perfect enough," like my cobra pose—not without flaw or fault, but aiming to be full, complete.

Home after yoga, I looked up what British pediatrician turned psychoanalyst D. W. Winnicott, who coined the phrase "good enough mother," had to say.

He didn't talk about starting a three-year-old with Suzuki violin lessons, ensuring that my eight-year-old never ever has to wear a dirty soccer uniform to a game, or buying your teen the designer clothing and big-screen TV everyone else has. Winnicott's prescription was *devotion*—abiding, affectionate attention. *Lead with your heart.* He maintained that every infant needs a mother whose faithful care literally keeps her baby alive. Then as the child grows and develops, the mother, in a natural way, meets her youngster's needs less completely, thereby allowing the child's self to emerge.

This is what Winnicott meant by "good enough." Too little devotion and the infant cannot live, too much devotion as the child grows and you stifle him. And we're more likely to hit that just-right dose if our intentions point high. Were Winnicott with us today, I think he would look at what's become of "good enough" and write instead of the "perfect enough mother."

By ditching "good enough mother" we throw out the second-rate implications that now go with it, dragging us down. Just thinking of myself as the "perfect enough mother" makes me stand a little straighter, step a bit more firmly.

With all this in mind, I began to move through my days of juggling the tasks and concerns of motherhood, aware of that contribution Winnicott saw in my daily mothering. I began to see that the distinction between "perfect enough" and falling short isn't in whether my children wear handmade Halloween constumes this year or whether the cupcakes for their birthday parties have sprinkles on them. It lies instead in my heart.

I've stopped asking myself, "Do I do enough?" I ask instead, "Do I lead with my heart?" Each of my days with my children embodies my dedication when I am open to them. Sitting around our kitchen table over dinner—whether it's packaged mac and cheese or roast beef with all the fixings—we are giving thanks, talking to each other, laughing, and I am demonstrating the dedicated care Winnicott spoke of. Are we mothers merely "good enough" who sacrifice, console, cajole, nourish, sustain, cherish, guide, shelter, and love, year after year? No. We are perfect enough.

The Imperfect Mom

MY PLAY DATE WITH THE DUCKS

Therese J. Borchard

If trauma is good for anything it makes for great conversational bits at the public park. And in between the covers of books.

That is how this collection emerged—out of a potentially tragic event, one that was publicized on the front page of the *Annapolis Capital*, forcing moms I hadn't met before out of their hiding places to console me with their confessions of just as bad, sometimes even worse, mishaps.

As the official winner of the Mortified Mom Award I became the renowned sympathetic ear to hundreds of other moms plagued with guilt, a local celebrity unintentionally soliciting tales of near-death, neglect, regret, remorse, and all that great stuff usually broadcast on Oprah shows.

Intrigued and fascinated and relieved by other mom's stories, I pursued even more of them with the hope that one day I would have a collection of stories that might shed some of the unnecessary weight shouldered by most moms in our society.

Not that I wanted in any way to celebrate sloppy mothering or glorify reckless and indifferent parenting. Instead I aspired to initiate a conversation, like the spontaneous ones that have happened at the coffee shop, parks, and street corners where I hang out with my two kids.

Ash Wednesday of 2004 was a holy day for me. Because the boy under my care could have easily died had his guardian angel not been eating sushi on the edge of the city dock in Annapolis, a picturesque setting where the Spa Creek of the Chesapeake Bay meets the quaint downtown shops.

A fellow preschool mom asked if I'd take her two-and-a-half-year-old, Will, for an hour or two so that she could run to the gym to tell some woman to pump more iron and run faster. Stacey is a physical trainer who usually uses the child-care center at the facility, but rumors of lice made her seek an alternative for this day. (Her son would have been better off with lice.)

I was partially relieved at her request, because I wanted to contribute an act of charity on Ash Wednesday, something easier than dragging my two-and-a-half-year-old son, David, and four-month-old daughter, Katherine, to church.

"No problem," I said, as I strapped her son's car seat between my son and my daughter. "It'll be fun. We'll get lunch, ice cream, and then feed the ducks."

It was a perfect day for that: sunny and in the forties. So after Will and David fueled up on sugar (mistake number one), we headed to the harbor to feed the ducks what was left of the boys' grilled cheese sandwiches. I had Katherine strapped onto me in order to manage the quick movements of the two-year-olds with both my hands, which is why I couldn't do anything but scream when David pushed Will into the frigid water of the creek, which was at least fifteen feet deep. As I frantically tried to unstrap Katherine from my chest, a man sitting nearby dove into the water and rescued Will.

I couldn't have lucked out more. A former lifeguard, Chris LaPanta had swum the polar bear swim competition in his hometown of Duluth, Minnesota. By the time I had one strap off my shoulder, my angel with cowboy boots on his feet and ashes on his forehead held Will with one hand and was swimming with him toward the nearest ladder.

The rest of the afternoon played out like a bad episode of *ER*. Although most of it was a blur, I can recall a few details: two restaurant owners stripping little Will and forty-one-year-old Chris of their glacial clothes to prevent hypothermia and wrapping each in white tablecloths; Chris's white briefs baking in the rotisserie at the poultry joint downtown while the locals commented on his chiseled six-pack abs; David screaming at Will because I had given the blue-lipped boy my son's winter coat, and then demanding to ride in the "fun truck" (ambulance) with his friend, not in Mom's gold sedan with no lights and sirens.

Mostly I remember asking myself what I was going to say to Stacey. I had begged her a few times to let me take Will since she seemed a bit stressed, and as the professional people-pleaser that I am, it was my responsibility to relieve her. We weren't great friends. We hadn't even made it beyond preschool small talk.

Question after question fired off in my mind: How was I going to explain this mess? How did I manage to screw up this bad? What should I have done to prevent this fiasco? (Stayed home and watched cartoons? Stuck the baby in a stroller? Restrained my son with a harness?)

In the ten minutes it took me to drive from the duck's diner to the hospital, all my bad mommy moments flashed before me. I was only two and a half years into the game of parenting and embarrassed of my scorecard.

There were those countless times I let David cry it out at

four in the morning to try to teach him how to fall back to sleep on his own, not knowing he was suffering from a painful ear infection. Would he bill me for the shrink visits twenty years hence that would result from this neglect?

I should have eliminated caffeine completely from my diet during the first trimester of my pregnancy with Katherine. Maybe that was the cause of her irregular heartbeat. And why did I fly with her when she was a wee two months old? Did I really think her immune system could fight off the nasty bacterial infection she caught on the plane, which almost had her hospitalized?

Instead of checking e-mails and making business calls, I should have devoted every second of David's first two years to educational interaction, naming every damn thing I saw (apple, boat, tree), like a few of the annoying moms I met at the park. Had I not planted him in front of a Baby Einstein video occasionally to get a little work done or had him amuse himself with puzzles, blocks, and Legos, maybe he wouldn't be speech-delayed.

In fact, so immersed in my own world was I that one-year-old David had managed to wander into the utility closet to squirt tub and tile cleaner into his eyes while I was checking my voicemail. After I flushed out his eyes, a neighbor drove us to the emergency room since I hadn't a clue if he had swallowed the stuff. Five hours later I learned he was okay.

Yeah, loser mom, I was driving yet again to the ER, this time with a kid who wasn't even my own.

I was shaking and crying and practically hyperventilating as I tried to reach Stacey to explain that we had taken a little detour that would delay her son's drop off. Since I had conveniently forgotten my cell phone that day, I waited until our family of three landed safely at the waiting room of the hospital before making a beeline for the public phone, dialing her cell about twenty times only to hear the same message over again.

"Answer your phone, damn it!" I yelled under my breath.

"What street does Ms. Hopkins live on?" the nurse asks me with a phone to her ear.

Not fair. I had to page through the thick white pages for Stacey's home number, while the nurse had an efficient computer system to dial up the number. Like a contestant on *Jeopardy*, or *Who Wants to Lose a Friend?*, I glared at the woman in blue scrubs while my fingers frantically dialed Stacey's number trying to reach her before the hospital spilled the beans.

"We talked to her, and she is on her way," the nurse with a calm grin finally told me.

The good news about this whole story is that little Will was released from the hospital a few hours later in tiptop shape. He suffered an ear infection or two due to the polluted water at the city dock (and the fact that, having tubes in his ears, he was supposed to wear plugs if submerged in any water at all), but seems to attach no negative feelings to his afternoon with Ms. Therese.

Stacey arrived at the hospital with wet eyes and smudged mascara. Can you believe she went to hug me first, and then realized she had better first console her son? The most empathetic and forgiving woman I have ever met, she did not once judge me or condemn me for my lack of prudence on Ash Wednesday.

"Accidents happen, Therese," she said, hugging me with all the strength she had left after an afternoon of physical training. "It could have happened to anyone." A few hours later the

Hopkins family made an after-dinner field trip to our home to see how *we* were doing.

Yes, accidents happen. We read about them every day in the paper. A truck plummets off an overpass onto a busy highway at rush hour, killing people in the cars below. A water taxi capsizes in gusty winds, leaving twenty-five people stranded in the water.

But when accidents happen to moms, we feel responsible. And very, very guilty.

I've heard my share of mom horror stories since everyone read about my afternoon with the ducks, which was printed on my birthday (no less).

A good friend of mine didn't mean to give her two kids food poisoning when she fed them bad meatballs, which they threw up for a day and a half. Another friend turned her back for a second to find her two-year-old at the bottom of some stairs with a broken arm.

My mom told me about a friend of hers who was building a snowman with her son. She ran into the house to fetch him a hat, and when she returned she couldn't find him because he had disappeared under a snowdrift, eventually freezing to death.

Of course there are also a variety of non-life-threatening regrets: the mother who thinks her decision to go back to work created a son with special needs; or the mom who finds her absolute devotion to her kids during their younger years has left her washed up, incapable of any passion or ambition of her own, now that she has time to herself. One woman feared her strict parenting style might cause her daughter to rebel as a teenager—in promiscuity or an eating disorder—and another is afraid her relaxed household might rear a hippie son who smokes too much dope and never takes responsibility for himself.

The timing of my big debut as Imperfect Mom couldn't have been more ironic. A month before the release of my new book entitled *I Love Being a Mom*, I was psyching myself up to utter sappy-sweet sound bites about the nothing-but-happy moments of motherhood. Still feeling the euphoria of my epidural and narcotics offered (okay, demanded) at my C-section, I entitled the last part of the book "Stretch Marks on My Heart."

There is no denying that my heart has expanded with the first eight pounds of love, and then the second seven, transforming me from a somewhat selfish writer and editor into a compassionate Mother Teresa who can occasionally change a diarrhea diaper without uttering a profanity and find my cell phone in the microwave without wanting to throw it at the little boy who hid it there.

However, I am now suffering the physical and emotional consequences of that heart enlargement, with stretch marks everywhere else to prove it. Dark circles under my eyes advertise my children's sleep schedule, and coughing attacks and green snot showcase the last infection that attacked our household.

When I called up an editor at a local parenting magazine about featuring a piece on my book, she responded with a pregnant pause.

"I don't want you to take this the wrong way, Therese." she said, "But, having been through the recent incident at the dock, would you ever consider writing a piece on being an imperfect mom?"

I almost hung up. I was already flashing her the bird. But then I had one of those thoughts that would make my father, the savvy businessman, very proud.

If people read the story and felt sorry for me, maybe they would buy my book.

"Uh. I guess I could do that. Sure," I said, hushing my ego, which wanted to direct her to a steamy place without lemonade stands.

"You're not going to write it, are you?" asked my husband, who knows what I'm thinking before I've had a chance to think it.

"Don't stoop that low. You're a good mom. A great mom," he said.

"It's not about being a good mom," I explained. "It's about not being perfect. And besides selling a few copies of my book, maybe some other mom will sleep a little better knowing she's not the only one who beats herself up and has messed up from time to time."

The piece, "Confessions of an Imperfect Mom," further established me as the all-too-human mom who admits it and who won't judge you if you have almost killed your kids or someone else's.

Moms surfaced everywhere I went with their tales of imperfection. At the pool (where my kids now don bright life jackets), moms confessed every kind of water horror story I'd ever like to know; at the park, they told me about jungle gyms gone bad and swings that bite the dust; and at street corners, stories about close calls with cars and bikes and trucks.

But more meaningful to me than the accounts of everything that could possibly go wrong, and everything you could worry about, were the candid tears, strong bear hugs, and sharp fears and regrets shared by the perfectionist moms among us who demand of themselves nothing short of a ten-point score.

One mom admitted to bawling at her office desk, exhausted and torn between pursuing a career that satisfies and stimulates her but steals time away from the little faces Scotch-taped to her computer monitor. Another recounted the sheer rage she feels when her daughter's bedtime routine takes an extra half-hour, eating away minutes from her coveted and nearly extinct personal time.

When I sent word out to writer and editor friends that I was looking for imperfect mom stories, my e-mail inbox was instantly flooded with confessions of all sorts. Some themes emerged, which make up the sections of this book.

In the first part, writers lament events and incidents that caused a kind of false start into motherhood. Award-winning novelist Caroline Leavitt tells of the traumatic first year of her son's life, in which she fell critically ill and nearly died. Unable to hold her infant for the first six months, the road to a loving relationship involved its share of work and patience. Former *Working Mother* executive editor Gail Belsky recounts the emotional torture that led to the secret circumcision of her son. Freelance writer Maria Rodriquez divulges her "failure" at labor that resulted in a planned C-section. The Imperfect Parent Web site cocreator Jessica Carlson relates the scary birth of her premature son. Freelance writer Kelly Johnson Harrington crafts a somber but important piece on her multiple miscarriages. And writer-activist Asra Nomani sounds off against critics who see her, an unwed mother, as a criminal in the eyes of Pakistan's Islamic law.

The second section includes a variety of near-miss stories,

like veteran journalist Judith Newman's accident that landed her and her twins in the emergency room; bestselling author Andrea Buchanan's story on how a pile of dirty laundry saved her son's life when he fell from the changing table; award-winning novelist Gayle Brandeis's tale of the camping trip from hell; *Ladies' Home Journal* deputy editor Margo Gilman's harrowing details of the time her daughter fell fifteen feet onto a brick patio and survived; and Beliefnet managing editor Wendy Schuman's hair-raising tale of the afternoon she and her daughter took a wrong step onto a steep ledge on a highway overpass.

A third set of essays offers a selection of lighter testimonies, replete with humorous misgivings of every kind. Like bestselling memoirist Helene Stapinski's piece on the week she and her lactating breasts took off on her husband and son, leaving both high and dry, as she did shots at an old bar with a friend. Or *American Baby* managing editor Kate Kelly's hilarious argument on why tadpoles don't make great house pets. *Philadelphia Daily News* columnist Ronnie Polaneczky comically relates her afternoon tea at the Four Seasons Hotel, "shrink insurance" she calls it, for the time her daughter fainted while mommy gave blood. Bestselling author Muffy Mead-Ferro confesses to her slacker summer, three months without one organized activity. *Real Simple* senior editor Jenny Rosenstrach offers the resolution she and her husband made after one "Itsy Bitsy Spider" song too many. And author and zine publisher Ayun Halliday depicts the bizarre and intense catfights that went down on a discussion board of a parenting Web site.

The fourth group of essays highlights all the grayness coloring motherhood, like the constant lowering of the culinary (and nutritious) bar, as *Salon* Table Talk host Mary Elizabeth Williams describes it, from breast milk for her infant to handfuls of M&Ms for her four-year-old; the "camp angst" that has *Boston Globe* columnist Louise Kennedy wondering when to pull her six-year-old son from such fun as kids' archery and treks through poison ivy; *Redbook* contributing editor Shana Aborn's dilemma of how far to go in childproofing your home; Trish Dalton's decision to keep working, even if it means missing her daughter's birthday celebration at day care; the nearly impossible balancing act that *Baltimore Sun* columnist Susan Reimer performs daily in order to love her children equally but differently; and novelist Pamela Redbook Satran's argument on how becoming assertively imperfect has made her a better mom.

In Part V of this book, contributors expound on certain dreams gone awry, everything from getting expelled from carpool when losing a husband and a bit of sanity, in bestselling author Jacquelyn Mitchard's amusing but poignant piece, to accusations of being too lenient from the type-A neighbor who seems to have it more together, told with humor in Beliefnet senior editor Deborah Caldwell's essay. *Working Mother* contributing editor Katherine Lee expresses the guilt she feels for not choosing a better mate; *Canary Times* editor Teme Weinstein Ring describes the frustrating effects of chronic fatigue syndrome on mothering her two sons; and *Ladies' Home Journal* editor Nancy Bilyeau sorts out her questions and fears on raising a son with special needs.

The last section of pieces concentrates on generalized regrets of the past. Award-winning novelist Katherine Weber writes on not fighting back hard enough against the harmful message of our culture's media when her kids were preteens. Freelance writer Gabrielle Erickson wishes she hadn't cared so much about doing things the right and perfect way, and instead taught her kids a few more practical life skills. Novelist Rochelle Shapiro explains where she went wrong in overmothering her daughter. Baby Einstein creator Julie Aigner-Clark pens a beautiful piece on missed time and opportunities with her two daughters. And *Ladies' Home Journal* editor Lorraine Glennon assumes responsibility for a can-opener-impaired teenager.

The book opens and closes with two important essays. In her foreword, award-winning journalist Kathryn Black tells moms to ditch the term "good enough mother" and replace it with the kinder and more accurate "perfect enough mother." And in the epilogue, bestselling novelist and *Child* columnist Suzanne Finnamore toasts the readers in a much-needed celebration of imperfection.

What I have aimed for in this diverse collection of writings by new moms to veteran moms, humorists to memoirists to novelists, is a kind of support group in print for women with secret misgivings they take to bed. From amusing accounts of bad mommy moments to contrite confessions of regret, the essays compiled in this book, I hope, will make moms everywhere breathe a sigh of relief and relinquish their pursuit of perfection. Because there is no such thing as a perfect mom.

Part I: False Start

Two o'clock in the morning courage:
I mean unprepared courage.

— NAPOLEON

Caroline Leavitt

It's Christmastime. A shiny bright apple of a day in San Francisco and the three of us—me, my husband, Jeff, and our one-year-old son, Max—are at a concert. Max's in red corduroy overalls and a striped shirt, his hair long and golden as the day ahead of us. The concert's been going on for an hour already and the whole time Max has been contentedly sitting on his father's lap, so enthralled by the music, he seems hypnotized. Already, a woman has come over to compliment us on our well-behaved baby. "What a love!" she coos, chucking Max under the chin. Someone else crouches and snaps his picture. And then Jeff quietly looks at me and says "I have to pee."

We both know what that means. He quietly lifts Max up and sets him on my lap, and startled, Max looks wildly around. Jeff hastens to the bathroom, and almost as if on cue, Max begins to scream.

He wails when I try to rock him. He tries to peel himself off my body when I croon. And when I stand, trying to gently dance with him, he flails his hands. "Is he okay?" the person next to us asks with great concern, and I nod. "Colic," I lie, my mouth quivering. "A little stomach bug." I try to walk with Max, just to get away from all the concerned stares, and then suddenly there's Jeff, who takes Max again, and all the crying stops. We all sit back down, and even if no one is looking at us, I feel as though they are, and I feel as if I've failed, as if I'm some terrible monster of a mother that my own son screams when I try to hold him.

I halfheartedly hand Max a pacifier and he swats it out of my hand. "Fine," I snap. "Do without."

Jeff blinks at me. "He's a baby," he says quietly. "You know better."

I did know better. I knew that for the first three months of Max's life, I was critically ill and in a hospital, so all the bonding we were supposed to have just never happened. I knew that for the next three months I was still too sick to hold him, to feed him, to do more than talk to him and that, despite what magazines say, babies can recognize their moms by scent. This particular baby was more likely to recognize his blanket than he was me. The truth was, I didn't really know him. He didn't really know me. And what's more, he didn't seem to like me and I hadn't a clue what to do about it other than to sometimes, to my great shame and bewilderment, not like him back.

I tried but I wasn't always a good mother. I didn't look the part, bloated from the steroids I had to take for my illness, my skin gray, my hair falling out. To bond with him, I began to care for him, changing his diapers when he'd let me, giving him his bottle because I was too sick to breast-feed. One day, I was leaning over him, tickling him with my hair trying to get him to laugh, when a hank of my hair slid off, dusting his belly. Horrified, I grabbed for the hair the same time Max did, and jerked it out of his hand so hard he whimpered, and within minutes, we both were weeping.

Jeff soothed me. My friends soothed me. "Mothering is exhausting," a friend told me. "One day I was so tired, I put Sammy in the laundry hamper and left him there." She quickly added, "But I took him right out. Don't be so hard on yourself."

How could I not be?

It was Jeff who pushed us together, who made himself scarce. Max, of course, wasn't happy, which in turn, made me tense. But I was determined. I tried to do all the right things, to read to him, to splash him in his bath, to keep a smile on my face. One day, when I was reading to him, we both fell asleep on the bed together, and when we woke, we were gazing into each other's eyes, and I felt the shock of connection, and then, he lifted his small hand, like a starfish, and laid it against my cheek. He snuggled against me, and though I wasn't sleepy anymore, you couldn't have moved me with a forklift.

The great myth is that mother love comes instantly, as natural as breathing. Oh, maybe it does, for the lucky ones. All I know is, as they say, "We wuz robbed," Max and me. I missed out on the first few months, the plans I had had to read to him, to talk with him, the time I had arranged to be no one's but his. And he missed out, too. He had the adoration of his dad and his grandmothers, and a devoted baby nurse. But he didn't have me. And when we got to have each other, we each found a stranger in our midst. We both had to grapple with a person you get to know, you come to love. You realize you can no more do without them than you can without the oxygen you breathe.

Max is eight now. We spend almost all our time together and I take nothing for granted. I listen to him. I make him laugh. I watch him sleep. And every time he calls for me or seeks me out or takes my hand, I feel undone by my happiness. We're the love of each other's lives and I know the struggle it took to get there; I know what it cost both of us, and maybe that's what makes it all the more sweet.

Maria Rodriquez

I wasn't over the imperfect birth of my first son, as a planned cesarean, when I learned that my second child was sitting breech
position in my womb at eight months pregnant. Although the
C-section resulted in a healthy, six-pound baby boy, I still felt
gypped of my dream of a natural, vaginal birth in a birthing center with my baby's father cutting his umbilical cord.

The first time around, I failed miserably at all my attempts
to turn the little guy's head down. Nothing worked. Not even
my constant flips at the swimming pool, or my lying on the
ironing board upside down for half an hour every day. A
screaming baby arrived from behind the blue drapes hiding my
split-open belly. I could only kiss him and rub my cheek against
his for my arms were tied to the operating table.

This birth of my first son had taught me, at the gut level, that
not everything in my life was under my control. Since I saw my
second pregnancy as a chance to finally make things right, I
was devastated upon learning that I should not attempt to deliver baby number two vaginally either. Following my doctor's
instructions, I scheduled a cesarean at the hospital. And I was
even more terrified, because in addition to the recovery of a

major operation, I'd have a toddler running around the apartment.

Still, I did not give up. In my search for the perfect delivery, I read plenty of material to better understand the breech presentation, and why it happens. Some experts believed that it could be a result of tension held in the mother's lower abdomen, caused by excessive fear over something.

I spent hours at night wondering what exactly scared me so much. So many things bothered me. How could I find *the* one, that magical point that could transform me into the perfect pregnant woman? Clearly, something needed fixing, but I could not pinpoint what it was. In a bizarre twist of my mind, I began to consider my inability to carry the babies properly as a testament to my many failures, to my sheer imperfection.

I would have continued my pointless wondering in this mental world had it not been for my cheerful toddler and the most unreasonable urge to nest. As the beautiful weather approached, I was busy walking my one-year-old to the park, picking up daisies and bugs, cleaning the sand from his toys. I cleaned up the apartment, changed around the rooms, did a lot of groceries and laundry, sent lots of parcels with birthday presents and notes to our friends, and made new curtains. At night, as I lay exhausted on my bed, I touched my huge belly and felt my baby's head up close to my heart and his little feet kicking softly down my pelvis. This all kept me grounded and connected to the real world.

It was in the middle of one of these busy summer days when I climbed down from a city bus, waddling onto the sidewalk. A strong breath of air caressed my face, messed up my hair, and draped my blouse softly around my belly. Caught by surprise by my reflection in the mirror, I smiled. Strangely enough, I suddenly felt lightness in everything around me. For a moment I was a little girl giggling and skipping down the street saying out loud, "So what??"

"So what if I cannot find the missing piece in the breech baby puzzle?"

"So what if the baby is born by cesarean?"

"So what if I am so imperfect?"

"I am happy being here, being myself, carrying this little baby inside of me."

That night I felt an irresistible urge to write a letter. To whom I didn't know, but it was one of rage: against myself and against my own imperfect mom. As I contemplated my relationship with my mom, so much anger and pain surfaced. But then I began to envision her as a little girl, crying by herself in a room where the noise of my grandma's sewing machine was all she could hear. And then I saw my imperfect grandmother, making a wholehearted attempt to support her eight children, running up and down the house trying to make ends meet.

I cried for a long time, acknowledging all the love used up in trying be good mothers. At the end of the night, my desk was covered with stories of imperfect mothers woven together: their mistakes, vices, and love twined onto a fine thread woven down to my own experience with my sons.

The next morning I went to visit my midwife. As she massaged my back to release tension that day, she noticed more room in my pelvis. She said my body was ready, and began to try to turn the baby inside of me. He responded and positioned his head down the birth canal, in preparation for a natural birth.

When the happy moment of the birth arrived, we were all there: my deceased grandma, my mother living an ocean away, and myself. We were breeding life, and I embraced our imperfection as I did my new son.

Jessica Carlson

As if pregnancy weren't uncomfortable enough, Mother Nature and her twisted sense of humor blessed me in my third trimester with a case of bronchitis, complete with violent coughing spasms. This, combined with my ongoing battle with insomnia, deprived me of much needed rest. One late night, while plopped in my favorite chair, I had another hacking fit. As I reached up to cover my mouth, I felt a warm gush between my legs. A sickening feeling washed over me, as I had experienced water rupture with my first child and knew instinctively what had happened. I scrambled for the phone and called my ob-gyn. I was connected to his answering service (not surprising, as it was midnight), which blandly took my message and said they would page the doctor and have him call me. "Make it sooner than later," I muttered while hanging up the phone.

I rushed upstairs, shook my husband awake and explained that my water broke, and I needed to go to the hospital. He barely stirred—the seriousness of my words did not register in his groggy state. He was not in the high alert mode of most fathers-to-be, no clichéd bag packed and waiting by the front door, to be ready at a moment's notice. Why was he not immediately springing out of bed? Why was he not already out in the garage, warming up the car? Because it's eight weeks early, that's why, I reminded myself. Rousing him again, he questioned my diagnosis.

"Don't pregnant women have bladder issues? Maybe that's what this is," he said.

"I think I would know if I had only wet my pants," I growled, my irritation increasing exponentially.

"Yeah, but I remember reading something about—"

He noticed my hands moving to wrap around his neck.

"I'll get ready to go."

Just then the phone rang. It was my doctor. As I was explaining what happened, he interrupted me and asked to remind him how far along I was.

"Thirty-two weeks."

"Are you sure?"

Oh, gee, now that you ask, ha, ha, silly me, I thought it was December, not February—of course I'm sure, are you kidding me?!

"Yes, I'm sure," I said with great restraint.

I was waiting for him to comfort me, perhaps tell me that this happened more often than you would think—we can fill your amniotic sac up with saline, pop a cork in there, and you can go back home! But instead he said the words that I already knew in my heart, but was hoping not to hear.

"Go to the emergency room right now. You're going to deliver this baby."

I've always been a procrastinator. I'm sure it is a deeprooted subconscious rebelling against authority—I'll reluctantly conform and follow The Man's rigid timetables, but I'll be damned if he gets it early. Certainly a better explanation than simply being lazy. I only work my best when chasing a deadline. In college, papers and exams were always preceded by a late night fueled by coffee and cigarettes. At the office, I was the one standing by the printer, looking at my watch, waiting for the last pages of the report I had completed minutes before the big meeting. These words you are reading right now sneaked in just under the wire. Favor-seeking friends who append their requests with "whenever you get a chance," receive my warning that they need to pin down a date, don't worry about decorum, if they ever want the deed completed. I am the exception to the rule that slow and steady wins the race. I am Indiana Jones, just making it out of the cave before the big stone door crashes down, still managing to grab my hat.

As such, having my timetable shifted and heading to the delivery ward two months early threw me into a panic attack—not only because of the concern for the health of my child, but because I was not emotionally or physically ready to have this baby. Procrastination and premature birth are not two things that go together. I had not even thought about things that some women take care of before the zygote stage. Child care? Nothing lined up. My mother's promise to come visit when the baby was born? I hadn't even made the plane reservation yet. I had purchased a total of zero items in preparation of the baby. The unassembled crib was buried deep within our storage unit. Dirty laundry was piled in the basement. A myriad of things at work needed to be wrapped up before even thinking about maternity leave. I had not even made arrangements for someone to stay with my older son while I was giving birth. It looked as if my bad habit was finally biting me in the behind.

So when the doctors told me that the baby and I were stable and that they were delaying the C-section to begin steroid treatment to help my son's lungs develop, I was relieved not only that he would have a better chance for survival, but also because I could put off birth for another twenty-four hours. I felt a wave of relief, and having been given this new deadline, I was able to kick into high gear. I rapidly dictated instructions. Phone calls were made, voicemails left. My husband was able to go home to pack my bag and favorite pillow. My best friend agreed to drop everything to stay at our house through the delivery. It was all coming together.

My son, fully packed with my genes, has picked up my traits. He procrastinated for two weeks in the neonatal intensive care unit before being released from the hospital. Bittersweet, as I ached to have him home in my arms, but it did allow me to make a cart-stuffing trip to Target for supplies, and get his nursery together—the last screw went into the crib thirty minutes before he was scheduled to come home, of course.

He continues the procrastinating to this day—he's currently behind with his speech and developmental milestones. But I take it in stride confident that, like his mama, he's just biding his time, waiting for the clock to strike the eleventh hour before making his move.

THE SECRET CIRCUMCISION

Gail Belsky

I was a total nut job when my son was circumcised, but at least I had an excuse: my husband, Julian, had just betrayed me. Julian, on the other hand, was just plain insane.

Our unraveling began that first afternoon, as father and son bonded in the hospital chair. Julian held the baby in one hand and a baby-naming book in the other. (The fact that we still couldn't agree on a name didn't bode well.) I was just dozing off when the door swung open and the obstetrician came in, along with a nurse and a medical student. They'd come for the baby, as scheduled. But as the doctor moved toward the chair to get him, Julian turned a sick shade of white. Without a word, he dropped the book on the floor and clutched William to his chest.

I started to panic. What was he doing? The doctor wanted to know, too. The head of ob-gyn, she was only performing this circumcision because I had begged her to. Now she was standing in the middle of our room, watching Daddy have some sort of episode. Having none of it, she reached out for the baby. Julian tightened his grip.

The doctor turned to me. What was wrong with us, she demanded. We'd had months to figure this out.

True enough, but we'd spent most of them avoiding the subject. Circumcision was a loaded issue for both of us. I am Jewish, and while I hated the idea of hurting innocent babies, I couldn't break with tradition. Plus, if I had, it would have killed my mother. Julian is British, and he didn't think mutilation was necessary. He wanted to spare his son needless pain and suffering. If he hadn't, his father would have killed him.

I had another problem, one I didn't share with Julian or anyone else because they would have put me away: I felt doomed. We already had one happy, healthy child; how could I possibly have another? And while I wanted this baby desperately, I was weepy and ambivalent throughout the pregnancy, second-guessing myself every step of the way. William was already my baby of indecision.

By the time he was born, I expected to feel this way forever (a self-fulfilling prophecy, as it turned out). But I didn't think I'd disintegrate on the very first day—and certainly not over the baby's circumcision. Why would I? Julian and I were on the same page now: we would have the procedure done in the hospital, without ceremony or grandparents. So when I saw him pulling a Kramer on the doctor, I was so shocked I didn't know what to say. Thankfully, the doctor wasn't going to waste another minute waiting for a response. She said she would come back in the morning after we'd had a chance to get a grip on ourselves.

The door shut behind her, and for a moment it was quiet. But as soon as Julian opened his mouth, I started to sob. He was sorry, he said. He didn't know what came over him. Don't worry; he was sure he'd be fine in the morning.

I nodded, not at all sure. Then I let loose through the tears:

How could he do this to me? Why couldn't we ever stick to-gether? We'd made a decision, how could he go back on it?

Round and round we went, for more than four hours. William nursed twice and pooped once. Our special filet mignon dinner for two sat untouched on the tray. Julian tried to put me at ease: He could handle the circumcision now. He really did understand how important it was to me.

But I wasn't sure I understood anymore. I felt like a butcher. Our baby was perfect; how could I think of harming that beautiful little body? Now I was the irrational one, crying and carrying on with no ability to stop myself.

When the doctor showed up the next morning, Julian once again had William in the chair. She asked straight out: Are you ready this time? I nodded and turned to Julian. He didn't nod. Or speak. He just sat there, gripping the baby as he had the day before. The doctor and I both stared at him in disbelief, but deep down, I'm sure neither one of us thought he'd go through with it. This time the doctor was sympathetic; she sat next to Julian and told him a story about her brother back in India and the circumcision dilemma he had faced. She patted Julian's knee. Go home and be with your son, she said.

As miserable as I was, I couldn't let go either. I grabbed her arm. What if we change our minds? Could she still circumcise the baby? The answer was a reluctant yes: if I called her in the next day or two, she would figure out a way to do it. In the meantime, I needed to have quiet time with Julian and the baby.

We took William home the next day in near total silence. I couldn't believe I'd brought a baby into such a dysfunctional home—but I shouldn't have been so surprised. Wasn't this exactly what I feared would happen? We fooled everyone with our first child, but this baby had exposed us for the loser parents we were. We couldn't agree, we couldn't communicate, and worse yet, we couldn't come together for William. What kind of mother let things go this far? If Julian couldn't deal, why didn't I? There was nothing to say.

That night, lying in bed with the bassinet at our feet, I was finally able to speak to Julian. What was it, exactly, that upset him so much? The answer was surprisingly simple: He didn't mind if William were circumcised, he just couldn't be a party to it.

I was relieved, but depressed. We could have avoided this whole mess. If Julian had been more honest, if we had been more open, if I had been more grounded, we would have arrived here together. Instead, I would be going it alone.

I called the doctor in the morning. She told me to wait by the phone and be ready to rush back in at a minute's notice. The call came the next day. I put William in his infant car seat, eased my sorry self into the car, and drove forty minutes to the hospital. I told no one we were going; I was too sad and embarrassed. I thought of my mother, the calmest, surest parent alive. My indecision was excruciating to her, and yet she was solid and supportive throughout. (She did remind me once how important it was to her that William be circumcised, but that was it.)

I lugged my poor baby across the parking lot, up the street, and into the building, bleeding heavily from all the exertion. The doctor gave me hell: what was I doing carrying him on my own? She grabbed the car seat out of my hands and took off down the hall, with me hustling to keep up with her. She picked up a nurse on the way and ducked into a treatment room. I didn't realize it then, but she was breaking all the rules for me.

William was no longer a patient in the hospital; she had no legal right to treat him there.

I watched as the nurse strapped him down and swabbed his genitals. Then I stood outside the door and listened to him scream. I felt I owed him that much. But instead of making me more miserable, hearing his pain gave me a small measure of comfort. I was finally there for him. Somehow, I felt like more of a mother to him doing it this way than if I had sat in my hospital bed, waiting for him to be returned to me, all clean and neat, as if nothing had happened.

When they were done, the nurse gave me instructions for changing his dressing, cleaning the wound, and checking for signs of infection. If I hadn't been such a head case, William could have had a proper circumcision and professional follow-up care in the hospital. Now he was in the hands of a total incompetent—me. Before we left the hospital, I made a promise to myself: I would not beat myself up every time I changed his diaper. I would take care of it and move on.

When she found out I had done all this alone, my mother was upset. She would have gone with me. I tried to explain, and as usual, she seemed to understand. This was between William and me. I needed to find my footing with him and not feel like a total failure. I needed to take charge and make decisions without falling apart. He and I deserved it.

Kelly Harrington Johnson

"You come from a long line of fertile women," my mother said to me matter-of-factly. We were on our way home from the store. I couldn't have been more than twelve years old. But, even then, I sensed this was something special. I suspect she passed this information on to me not so much to instill a sense of pride as to ward off teenage hanky-panky. Still, it was something I relished knowing about myself.

My first two pregnancies seemed to prove this genetic predisposition. I conceived easily; I grew big, healthy babies; and I birthed them without complication. I nursed my boys and fed them organic food. I made friends with other mothers who shared my parenting philosophies. We swapped stories, attended one another's home births, and practiced homeopathy. Things were just as I had always imagined they would be.

In the summer of 1998, my husband and I decided it was time for baby number three. I became pregnant quickly; and then, ten weeks into the pregnancy, I miscarried. I could not believe it. More precisely, I could not believe it had happened to me. I worked through the grief and the loss well enough, I suppose. I even prided myself on how bravely I handled it. Two months later, having put the miscarriage behind me, it was back to makin' babies! Then the unthinkable happened. I miscarried again. And again. And again. All told, I would lose four pregnancies over the course of the year.

A wise person once said that hard times don't build character, they reveal it. Oh, I wish this weren't true. I had flown so high and long on paper wings, smug about what my body could do and secretly believing it somehow made me a good mother, that the fall to earth was inevitable.

Intellectually, of course, I understood that a miscarriage is nature's way of ending a pregnancy that is not developing normally. But the thought that I might never bear another child left me feeling utterly broken. I couldn't reconcile the mother I had been with the barren woman I seemed to have become. How could my body not know how to do this anymore, I wondered.

And always, in the back of my mind, were the whispers of the Good Mother, the unyielding archetype of maternal perfection: "Good Mothers have their babies," she taunted. "Their bodies know what to do to keep those babies inside."

Complicating matters was the fact that these were "only" miscarriages. I had not lost a living child. People were sorry for me, sure; but, the truth is, no one grieves a miscarriage the way a mother does. And it seemed to me I was expected to move on from these losses in a timely fashion. Determined not to overstep this boundary, I worked at accumulating a list of the many things for which I should have felt grateful.

Think of all the mothers whose children have cancer, I told myself. Think of the parents whose children have died! Think of your boys—aren't you grateful for them!?

And this is where I made a critical mistake. I thought I could shed the skin of failure by showing the world that the love I had for my boys was greater than the pain caused by the miscarriages.

"Yes," the Good Mother agreed. "A Good Mother's love for her children heals all wounds. It is always enough."

And so I took my grief and pushed it aside. I stuffed it down and force-fed myself gratitude, day in and day out. I told anyone who would listen about how my heart was so full of love for my children that I didn't really feel much grief when those babies bled out of me. Really. I don't. Really. And the grief dug down deeper.

And it did what any good wound will do when left unattended. It ravaged me from the inside out. I found out the hard way that when you deny grief its voice, it comes back at you with a vengeance. In my case, it reemerged as bitterness and rage. I was seething.

What kind of mother can't bear her own children! How dare this be taken from me! I couldn't stand the shame, the pitying glances, the judgments I was sure people were making about me. I wanted my unblemished motherhood back. I didn't want to be this broken half-mother anymore.

And then, in another terrible miscalculation, I allowed myself to begin to indulge petty, hurtful thoughts about the people in my life, and especially pregnant people. I started small, just a little nasty thought here and there to take the edge off. But it was like discovering a wonderful new drug. Little thoughts became big ones and before I knew it, they were my most loyal companions: "Look at my neighbor patting her barely pregnant belly. Ugh—I'd love to see her miscarry"; "Susie-Q is pregnant again, is she? She's already got five kids. A little miscarriage is just what she needs."

It was the most self-destructive thing I have ever done, and it was terribly isolating because these kinds of thoughts are dark secrets that must be kept. So I held them in and they roiled around in my mind and my soul. I was a mess.

The afternoon I realized I was about to suffer my third miscarriage, I called the assistant pastor at my church (a woman I hardly knew), and poured out my rage to her over the phone. I had stopped by her office earlier that week to say a prayer of thanks because this pregnancy, which had looked like it might not be viable, had come along. The doctors had found a heartbeat and I felt as though I had experienced some kind of miracle. So when, one week later, the bleeding started and didn't stop, my despair overwhelmed me.

I called Jenny, my mouth barely able to form the words, "I'm losing this one too." I don't remember what she said, only that it brought me some comfort; then I had to go and pick up my boys from preschool.

When I arrived home, I found in my doorjamb Jenny's business card with a note saying she had come by to be with me during this awful time. She closed by writing this: "There is nothing more painful to a mother than the loss of a child."

These words stunned me; I had to read them several times before they sunk in. She did not see me the way I saw myself: broken and pathetic. What she saw was a mother in terrible pain. By that point, it was inconceivable to me that anyone could hear my story and feel that I was someone who deserved this kind of care and attention. My litany of reasons to be grateful had long since claimed victory over my right to grieve. But there it was in my door, proof that on this day, in that moment, my loss and my grief were real, they mattered, and they needed tending to. I saw myself through her eyes . . . I saw things the way they were.

And I wept. I wept for all the grief I had denied. I wept for my shattered dreams. I wept for the children I would never hold in my arms.

I would go on to have one more miscarriage after this. But I grieved it. I grieved all my losses with this one, I think. And I began to reframe my picture of motherhood.

Motherhood is not simply about bringing babies into the world; it's about taking life on with arms wide open. I was a mother when I prayed night and day for the viability of the four cells God had sown together inside me. I was a mother when I dared to care for a life that fought to survive. I was a mother when I allowed myself to grieve a tiny heart that beat, valiantly at first, then more slowly, and that ultimately ceased. Somehow, from the wreckage of everything I thought I lost, came the mother I was meant to be.

Asra Q. Nomani

~~~~~~

It could be said I was an imperfect mother from the moment I conceived. I wasn't wearing a wedding ring. As if that wasn't bad enough, I was a criminal in the eyes of Pakistan's Islamic law.

An American born in India, I had gone to Pakistan after September 11, 2001, as a journalist for *Salon* magazine. I fell in love with a dashing young Muslim man as we waded in the waters of the Arabian Sea off the shores of the port city of Karachi. Over the next weeks of our romance, he told me he wanted to marry me. When I told him I was pregnant his talk of marriage disappeared. I had violated the Islamic law of Pakistan by committing *zina* or "illegal sex." My scarlet letter: Z. I was no longer the perfect bride. While my baby's father walked away from me and my swelling belly, I battled the shame of my imperfection. Similarly, mothers are disproportionately punished under Islamic sex laws; men very often deny their involvement and walk away scot-free.

When my son was born, wide-eyed and perfect, I was reborn. I gazed at the beautiful face of my son, whom I named Shibli, meaning "my lion cub," and asked myself: Could I be not just a good mother but a great mother despite my imperfection?

Others have tried to answer that question for me over the two-and-a-half years that my son has been on this earth, projecting their own prejudices and opinions upon me and my son, as I spoke throughout North America and wrote honestly in two books about my son's conception and my decision to raise him as a single mother.

On a progressive Muslim Web site one man wrote: "I believe the responsible thing to do would have been to give her child up for adoption so he could benefit from a two-parent home. Having children out of wedlock for whatever reason hurts the children and ultimately degrades the moral fabric of society."

Another reader on a spirituality and religion Web site, Beliefnet, raised the prospect of an evaluation report on me as a mother: "I am looking forward to another interview with this Muslim journalist five years from now. How is she raising her kid? What values is she instilling in him?" These challenges raised questions in my own mind about myself as a mother.

But I've discovered that the clearest answer comes from only one place: my son—the closest that I come to the divine. The answer has revealed itself in the most unexpected and unscripted of ways. But it sustains me in the darkest of moments.

On the eve of Mother's Day 2005, I found myself in one of those dark moments. I was sitting in a San Francisco hotel room on a cross-country trip that I called the Muslim Women's Freedom Tour. I had written a book, *Standing Alone in Mecca: An American Woman's Struggle for the Soul of Islam*, a manifesto of women's rights in Islam. I had taken my intimate confrontation with sexist, anti-women traditions perpetuated in the Muslim world to discover the truth of women's place in Islam. I had discovered that women are being denied rights Islam granted them in the seventh century, from the bedroom to the mosque, because of man-made rules used to essentially control them. On my Freedom Tour, I stormed mosques that forced women into basements and secluded rooms, and I organized the first publicly announced woman-led mixed-gender prayer of our modern day.

At that moment in San Francisco, I was thousands of miles away from my son, who was bouncing every night between my loving mother and father, who were caring for him while I was on the road. I felt guilty leaving my son. But a friend asked me: "Is he happy with your mother and father?" He was.

As I was considering my guilt, I received an e-mail from an elderly Muslim man in San Diego: "An Open Letter to Asra Nomani." He had read my book. He knew my story. He told me he and his wife were praying that I got married soon to "a nice Muslim man who adopts Shibli as his son." Okay, I thought. That's nice enough. I had advertised myself on Beliefnet's matchmaking service but had as yet made no love connections. I could use a little prayer.

But the man's logic stunned me. He said I had to get married "otherwise when Shibli grows old and cannot tell . . . his friends and school mates or put [his] father's name [on] . . . forms, he will be miserable and most likely condemn his mother." *Miserable?* I did a Google search. Sri Lankan victims of the tsunami were miserable after the tidal waves hit Asia. *Condemn?* Some families of U.S. soldiers condemned President Bush's war on Iraq. Irish newspapers condemned the murder of a journalist in Northern Ireland. A Florida man was condemned for the rape and strangulation of a widow. Was my son going to *condemn* me if I didn't get married? Was my son going to *condemn* me because he stayed with his grandparents instead of a father when I was on the road? Was my son going to be *miserable* because he didn't have a father in his life?

I pondered these questions as I returned home, wondering how my son would greet me. As I stepped before him, my son ran swiftly to me across the freshly mowed lawn, tumbling into my arms with a wide smile and twinkling eyes. Taking my hand, my son eagerly told me, "Close eyes, Mama." He led me around the back of my parents' house (not warning me of the pebbles under my bare feet).

"Open eyes!" he declared, waving his hand like a magic wand over a flower bed of violet foxgloves, red dahlias, yellow day lilies, and pink snapdragons he had planted with his grandfather's (small) help for Mother's Day.

"For Mama!" he declared proudly, as I opened my eyes and let them soak in the radiance of my son and his flowers in the sunshine.

I swept this bundle of joy into my arms, his grin widening with the growing press of my embrace.

"I love you, Shibli!" I sang from my heart.

"I love you, Mama!" he said, burying himself against me.

I had my answer.

Part II: Near Miss and Miss Again

Put all your eggs in the one basket,
and—WATCH THAT BASKET.

— MARK TWAIN

Margot Gilman

~~~~~~

When I tell this story, I usually cut right to the ending, to spare my audience any undue cliffhanger torment:

She lived. She'll be fine. With luck, she won't even have a memory of it.

But in those first harrowing moments, on a cloudless summer morning almost three years ago, a happy outcome seemed almost too much to hope for. Even now, it's a bit hard to write about. It was 11:00 a.m. on a Saturday in July, and Lily, our just-turned-two-year-old daughter, had been put down for a nap in her crib in an upstairs bedroom. Our family, which also includes our older daughter, Thea, then five, was at our weekend house in the country, about two hours away from where we live in New York City; we were expecting a houseful of company and were busy getting ready. Some of our guests had already arrived; they needed to be gotten drinks and shown where to put their bags. Wet bathing suits and towels still strewn about needed to be hung up to dry. Steve put Lily down for a nap partly because she needed one, partly because *we* needed *her*, just then, to be out of our hair.

It was my friend Rick who saw the *whoosh* out of the corner of his eye. He and I were talking in the living room, standing next to a set of French doors that lead out to the patio. "Lily," he said to me with no particular urgency, and pointed outside. I stepped through the doors, expecting to find Lily with a scraped knee or some other minor malady in need of a feel-better kiss. That she had been put down for a nap in her crib was something my brain, at that moment, wasn't processing. So when I saw her on the brick patio, on her back, eyes rolled back, not moving, it took me a beat to put it together. I looked up to the window of the bedroom with her crib, a good sixteen feet overhead, and saw that the bottom half of the screen was pushed out. "Oh my God!" I screamed. "Lily fell out of the window!"

From wherever he was in the house, Steve was by my side in an instant. He scooped Lily up in his arms. Through my terror, I remember thinking that he shouldn't have moved her, that that could actually worsen whatever injury she might have sustained. But Steve was going on instinct and his instinct was to hold her close.

Most of us are lucky enough to never know what sheer terror feels like. I never had—until the next agonizing few moments. The position of Lily's head seemed unnatural, as if it was rotated farther to the right than the bones should allow it to go. She was silent and perfectly still. The horrific possibilities of what we might be confronting—brain trauma, spinal cord injury, worse—so unfathomable, were suddenly real. I remember looking at Thea who was now standing, frozen, nearby. Watching her frantic parents, she knew that something very, very bad had happened and there was raw fear in her eyes. But it was Steve's eyes that mirrored my personal agony: the indescribable pain that comes from seeing your child gravely hurt, and feeling entirely responsible.

For there was no mystery to how Lily had managed to get up onto the sill of an open window and fall out. The crib she was supposed to be napping in was positioned along a wall with a swath of four windows, where it had always been. For two years, we walked past that crib and windowed wall many times a day, never once linking the two as a recipe for catastrophe, even on hot days, such as this one, when we kept the windows open. We knew about window guards—where we live in the city they are required by code, and we had one in every window of our ninth-floor apartment—but the thought of installing guards in the country had never occurred to us. Until that day in July Lily had never climbed out of her crib on her own, and since Thea had not singlehandedly surmounted her own crib's railing until the age of two and a half, we had not been anticipating Lily's precociousness.

But before Steve and I could contemplate our utter culpability too completely, Lily started to move her arms and legs. Then she started to cry: wrenching, bloodcurdling sobs. We knew this was good. Nine-one-one had been called, and after it was determined that Lily's limb movement obviated the need for a Medevac helicopter, an ambulance was dispatched. It arrived within minutes, as did two policemen, apparently sent to determine whether criminal neglect was a factor. The paramedics strapped Lily to a gurney, and rushed her to the hospital. I stayed with her in the ambulance and Steve followed in our car. I guess the policemen showed themselves out, satisfied that no arrests were in order. Thea stayed behind with the houseguests.

At the hospital, poor little Lily was given full-body X-rays and CAT scans. It took a few more harrowing hours before doctors told us that she was, despite a sixteen-foot tumble onto a hard brick surface, none the worse for wear. No broken bones, no internal bleeding, no brain damage, thank heavens. People don't believe me when I tell them this, but the child didn't even have a scrape or get a bruise. Steve and I have joked that she must have landed on her diaper, which lucky for us happened to have been very full. Friends have marveled at the possibility of angel's wings being involved, and have kiddingly suggested that her baby bones must have had some other-worldly rubber-to-calcium ratio. We'll never know how Lily managed to escape injury. It was, without doubt, a miracle.

Our daughter was fine, but over the next weeks and months it became clear that the hard part wasn't over. When they weren't sharing our relief or helping us find some inkling of humor, some friends and family saw fit to take our near-tragedy and rub our noses in it. While no one called us irresponsible parents to our face, clucking tongues found other ways of making themselves heard. There were wisecracks, like the one from a friend who rather mindlessly said she thought babies only fell out of windows of the homes of inner-city teenaged moms. There were overdramatized displays of playground hypervigilance—friends who hovered not around their child on the monkey bars, but *mine*. In the who's-a-better-mom competition that all mothers engage in to some extent, my having a daughter who had fallen out of a window branded me a C-minus student in need of remedial help.

To a large extent, I didn't blame them. If people were going to think of us as parental delinquents, I had to admit they had a pretty good case. God knows I blamed myself terribly—had Lily had really been hurt . . . well, I didn't know if I could have survived that. And I felt shame. At first, I hesitated to tell my Lily-out-the-window story for fear of the stigma. ("Oh, there goes Margot," I could just hear the mothers at my kids' school snickering. "Did you hear how her carelessness almost cost her daughter her life?") But perspective has a way of evolving with time and consideration, and little by little my attitude about the Lily episode—particularly my complicity—shifted. My crime, I realized, was failing to have seen danger around every corner. And I started to think maybe that's not such a terrible thing.

Of course, it's not as if I've ever been some kind of crazy risk monger. I buy into much of what parents do these days to make their children's lives lump and bump free: my kids use car seats, wear bike helmets, and are cautioned not to talk to strangers. But there's no denying that as a society we've taken parental paranoia to a ludicrous extreme. I see examples every day—parents who outfit their kids in body armor just to roller skate on the driveway, who pack sanitizing gels in their backpacks for them to use in school restrooms. I'm just not hardwired for that kind of worry—and now I'm not afraid to admit it. Nor do I share the illusion that as a parent you can have total control. Parents who try to grasp for it anyway are the ones who make *me* nervous, because their kids learn to be timid and fearful. Isn't a belief in their own invincibility one of the important lessons of childhood?

Today, two years later, Lily is an electric pinball of a four-year-old, one of those kids who loves to show off death-defying physical stunts, like jumping to the floor from the top of Daddy's shoulders or doing back flips off the arm of the sofa. Steve and I cheer her on, joking about how her rubbery bones keep coming in handy. She won't be falling out of any more windows—we learned our lesson and now open second-story windows only from the top. But she's growing up with a sense of her own powerful invulnerability—and we feel pretty good that we're doing our job.

Gayle Brandeis

~~~~~~

Joshua Tree National Monument is like another planet. Huge outcroppings of boulders spring from the flat desert floor— some look like wet sand dribbled from the hand of a giant; others are smooth and hulking as a giant's back. Some are so big you can barely see the rock climbers scaling their sides. The Joshua trees themselves, peppered throughout the park, look like shaggy, spiny creatures reaching for the sky. It's a most bizarre landscape, raw and brutal and gorgeous. A landscape that leaves me feeling slightly alien, slightly raw, myself. Especially this year.

My husband's family has a tradition of camping in Joshua Tree every Easter. I look forward to these trips with a mixture of excitement and dread; I am fascinated by Joshua Tree, but I am not much of a camper. I seem to have a genetic predisposition against sleeping in tents. I hate washing pots and pans out in the wilderness (I hate washing them in civilization, too, but somehow doing it outdoors makes the task seem even more odious). When we drive past the Oasis of Eden Inn on our way to the park, I am always tempted to forgo our campsite and book one of their caveman-themed rooms.

The kids, however, are always thrilled to go camping at

Joshua Tree. They love roasting marshmallows and scrambling over rocks and dying Easter eggs that immediately go sulfurous in the desert heat. Where they see fun, though, I often see danger. I worry that they're going to get bit by rattlesnakes or scorpions, that they're going to tumble into a bed of cactus spikes, that they're going to fall off a cliff or succumb to heatstroke. Silly me, I didn't think to worry about pretzels.

Pretzels, as we all know now, are dangerous buggers. They can bring the so-called leader of the free world to his knees (or, more accurately, to his face). Don't let Mr. Salty fool you with his jaunty cap and saucy grin. He's one bad mofo.

Shortly after we set up camp, my daughter Hannah wandered around the site checking things out, sucking the salt off a pretzel rod. I guess she wasn't exactly watching where she was going—one end of the rod bumped into a boulder; the other end went straight through the roof of her mouth. She screamed so loud, my husband, who had gone rock climbing several campsites over, felt as if she was shrieking directly in his ear. Blood poured from her mouth; she spit little bits of her palate onto the sand.

If I'm not predisposed to camping, I'm definitely not predisposed to handling my kids' injuries. I tend to freeze when they get hurt. I shut down. This is not a good thing. My kids come to me wanting help and comfort, and I stand there like a Joshua tree, my ineffectual arms raised to the sky. I also tend to get dizzy. All the blood drains from my head. It seems to drain from my body, too. I have no idea where my blood goes when something happens to my kids.

With some guidance from my less-paralyzed sister-in-law, I managed to clean out Hannah's mouth with bottled water and apply pressure with a paper towel until the bleeding stopped. I also managed to fling the gory pretzel against a rock face, shattering it into splinters. By the time my husband made it back to the campsite, both Hannah and I were nearly catatonic from the drama.

I was sure Hannah's palate would need stitches, but my husband, who keeps a blessedly clear head during disasters, determined she would be fine. And she was. Her mouth hurt a little bit when she ate salty foods—making pretzels doubly off-limits—but otherwise she barely noticed the gash the rest of the trip. I, however, had a harder time recovering. So when my son and my sister-in-law's boyfriend's kids got lost in the desert a few hours later, it was very easy to slip right back into catatonia. I sat like a stone while my husband and the boyfriend went off to search for them, while the enormous sky got darker and darker, while my mother-in-law brought me a bowl of homemade chili I could barely eat.

The year before, my husband and a friend were stranded overnight in the mountains after taking a wrong turn while mountain biking. The search and rescue team was unable to find them. I was so worried I couldn't stop throwing up and had to be taken to the hospital. When my son was lost, I was too numb to even feel nauseous.

The kids were found about an hour later, stuck on a rock ledge. By the time they were rescued and returned to the campsite I was so frozen it took a long time (and a lot of hugs from my children) for me to feel human again, to recognize the crazy pounding of my heart.

The next day, my period started a week early; no one in our group had any "feminine hygiene" products on hand, so I had to fashion pads out of wadded-up tissues and paper towels. It was a bit of a pain, but I didn't mind—after my spectacular ineptitude in the face of my kids' dramas, at least I knew I could be resourceful in certain situations.

I think back on our weekend now and wonder what happened to the shards from Hannah's pretzel. Maybe a fringe-toed lizard eventually ate them. Maybe they've worked their way into the desert floor, becoming one with the granite grit and the wild mustard. I hope I left my immobilization behind, too, let it sink into the boulders where it belongs. Maybe next year we can rent one of those caveman rooms. And we'll definitely leave the pretzels at home.

Judith Newman

My friend, an emergency-room surgeon, keeps a secret photo stash of his patients and the objects they've shoved up their bottoms. "Look!" he exclaims, for the pleasure of hearing me shriek at the sight of a man who's inserted a cabbage large enough to win a 4-H prize. "You'd be amazed how many objects people just 'slip and fall on in the shower'!"

I couldn't help thinking of this friend as I sat in my local ER on a sunny, bitterly cold January morning, clutching my ripped eyeball and cradling my two-year-old's blood-soaked head. This looked bad. Really bad. I'd better come up with a good story, because the truth was just too mortifying.

Yet it all came from love. Didn't it?

Perhaps I should backtrack. It is true I'm a little less safety-conscious than most mothers. Not that I don't *feel* that lurch in the stomach when I see one of my twin boys climb shakily to the tallest slide in the playground or catapult himself off the trampoline designed for bigger kids. But from the moment I was sliced open and my twin boys emerged, I made a promise to myself: I would not hover. I would not panic (at least, not visibly) at every fever, nor gasp at every fall. I would not, in other words, make my sons into the wuss my parents made me.

Don't get me wrong. My doting parents did everything right, with one exception: if they'd been allowed, they would have raised me in a plastic bubble. In my family, being unathletic and physically timorous were not traits to be gently worked through and perhaps overcome. They were practically points of pride: *Hey, my daughter may not be able to run a mile, but she read* War and Peace *when she was twelve!* When I was eleven I took up horseback riding. It was the only sport I've ever been passionate about, in that typical teen-girl, horse-is-as-close-as-I-dare-get-to-a-real-penis way. I had absolutely no natural talent, but certainly it did not help to have ones parents standing white-knuckled at the railing, screaming *Watch Out* every time another horse cantered by me. Eventually they were banned from my lessons, but not before I had received the indelible message: *Just getting out of bed is, for you, a hazard. It's astounding you still walk the earth.*

Still, being a brain-on-a-stick seemed fine to me until I reached my thirties and realized how much I would never experience. Camping? *Insects.* Climbing Machu Picchu? *Who needs to climb when I have the Discovery Channel?* I had never set out to become Woody Allen, but as I aged I began to feel increasingly anxious when I left Manhattan. In a sense, I had created my own plastic bubble and moved right in.

This was not the life I wanted for my boys.

Again, I don't want to overstate the case. I didn't sign them up for *Soldier of Fortune* the moment they left the NICU. But from the earliest age, there was not a peep from me when they rolled off the bed and onto the dog or fell or stabbed themselves in the head with a seemingly innocuous toy truck or injured themselves in the hundred mysterious ways toddlers manage to find. And I was constantly stopping my husband from gasping and rushing to scoop them up. A former rock-climber and power-lifter, John had lost all his front teeth when he was harpooned in the jaw by a guardrail he fell on while climbing the face of a old building that crumbled beneath him. So it's safe to say that *he* is not overly concerned with his own personal safety. Yet he would be much happier if Henry and Gus wore helmets until they were eighteen. We argued constantly, but I usually won out. If I couldn't be Tony Hawk myself, I'd raise a child who was.

Although . . . from the earliest age, my children were not fully cooperating with my plan. My twins are decidedly non-identical. Henry is the doppelgänger of my husband: loud and demanding—but also wildly affectionate, powerfully built and athletic. He is adventurous but judicious: he knows what he can do and what he can't. Augustus belies his name: tiny, sweet, contemplative, skinny, delicate, and—like Mom—utterly lacking in grace, muscle-tone, and depth perception. He's a man who will not run if he can walk, and will not walk if there's someone around to carry him. In fact, he barely needs arms—if I turn my back at dinner, his twin brother is feeding him.

Still, I treated them exactly the same. If Gus was naturally timorous, I just knew it was in my power to make him blossom into the adventurer I never was. And as for Henry . . . all would come naturally. Well, it would, if I could stop him from being so damn fastidious. For all his natural athleticism, he had inherited my aversion to dirt. How was he going to be camping out in the Atacama Desert if he screamed when he got sand between his toes?

All of which brings me back to the emergency room. It was seven in the morning, and I was still half asleep. Henry, in a rush of baby tenderness, had climbed into bed with me and reached over to hug my head like a boa constrictor. Instead, he somehow managed to graze my eyeball with his tiny sharp fingernail. The pain was like nothing I'd experienced before. But for reasons best known to myself, I decided I'd just let it ride, that if I ignored the pain for a little while it would go away. So instead of getting up and going to the doctor, I proceeded to play Torpedo, Henry's favorite early-morning game to play with me. Torpedo consisted of me hoisting him in the air and hurling him over my shoulder, into the middle of my king-sized bed. Only *this* king-sized bed was new; it had a wooden footboard the old bed didn't. And in *this* game of Torpedo, I was in pain and half blind.

I remember the cracking sound of Henry's skull meeting the wooden footboard, and the gush of blood over my bed. I remember John grabbing him, and grabbing me, and hustling us both into the cab to the nearest hospital. Gus had to come too, of course, wailing the whole way in empathy, or perhaps because the mere sight of a white coat is enough to set him off. I'm not quite sure what I babbled to the person who greeted us in the ER, though I was quite sure Henry's comment— "Mommy play Torpedo with me"—was going to bring out the lady from Child Protective Services.

John, Henry, and Gus went in one room, I went in another. My eyeball was sprayed with an anesthetic for which, to this day, I bless the gods. As I explained to the very bored (and, apparently, twelve-year-old) resident what had transpired, he picked the outer layer of ripped skin off my cornea. This is just as unpleasant as it sounds. Meanwhile Henry, in a room nearby, had long since stopped crying, and was instead having an animated discussion with the doctor about getting blood out of his T-shirt; knowing our anal-retentive child was a sucker for cleaning jobs, John had thoughtfully brought along the blood-stained T-shirt as a distraction, and together, while waiting for the doctor, they had been washing it out in the sink.

As it turns out, head wounds bleed a lot, even those that are relatively minor. Henry didn't need stitches. He's still, however, talking about the blood on the T-shirt.

So what has my little experience in confidence-building and encouraging athletic prowess wrought? In a word: Nothing. Nothing I have done in the past three and a half years seems to have made the slightest alteration in their innate personalities. A year after our ER visit, Henry still loves to play Torpedo, and can still leap like a stag over a mud puddle three times as long as he is—which is just as well, because if he ever actually got his foot wet in that mud puddle, he would probably have a heart attack. Augustus, who would happily bathe in the mud puddle, and who regularly finds dead waterbugs in our apartment basement and brings them to me, triumphantly, as gifts, still can barely bring himself to climb a few rungs of a playground ladder; his favorite mode of transportation is a cab and, failing that, my shoulders. Put them together, and they would make the daredevil I yearn for. As they are now . . . uh, not so much.

After my Torpedo incident with Henry, I comforted myself by saying that loving a child involves the two competing impulses of keeping them safe and letting them truly live. I still think this is true. But here's what's also true: we love them every day for who they are, not for who we want to be through them.

After all, what choice do we have?

Andrea Buchanan

~~~~~~~~~~~~~~~~~~~~~~~~~~~~~~~~~~~~~~~

I have a laundry problem. Well, maybe that's putting it too strongly: perhaps it is better to say I have "issues" with laundry. I'm not good with the taking-it-out-of-the-washer-and-putting-it-in-the-dryer-in-a-timely-fashion part; I'm not good with the taking-it-out-of-of-the-dryer-and-folding-it-up-in-a-timely-fashion part; I'm not good with the taking-the-folded-piles-and-putting-them-in-the-dresser-in-a-timely-fashion part. Right now as I type this, my laundry mocks me, from the wadded-up clean clothes that have yet to be folded on my bed, to the mounting basket of dirty clothes in the baby's room, to the wet clothes molding in the washer to the dry clothes wrinkling in the dryer. I am, I fear, laundry-impaired.

I'm aware, too, of the metaphor of laundry, and what my reluctance to deal with it means. I really do want to move on, I really do want to use what I already have, I really do want to take the things I've dirtied and make them clean again. And yet I fight against the dull repetition of it all: I want the triumph of things done and not the frustration of things undone. I find myself wishing futilely for everything to stay new, pristine, untouched by experience. When I see the laundry goading me from its solvenly lair atop the already full hamper or the basket or the table, I resent the way it represents all the things that change, the way the newness always fades, the need for decay and rebirth.

Self-cleaning clothes, I think: clothes that never need to be cleaned, that always stay new, intensely blue or perfectly creased. That's what I need. No laundry, ever—and perhaps with that, no need to deal with the way things change, with the importance of maintenance. The world opens up to me as I imagine it: dishes that no longer need washing, furniture that doesn't need dusting. I could be free from the drudgery that currently defines my life as a mother. Gleaming countertops, cat-hair-free carpet, fresh-smelling clothes; none of the defeating, endless cycle. None of the work.

Putting the laundry away, clearing the blue plastic basket to make room for the next load that waits in the dryer, I feel like Sisyphus, the man in the myth who was condemned to roll a huge boulder to the top of a mountain, whereupon it would roll back on him and he would have to repeat the effort again, for all of eternity. Stuffing the T-shirts in drawers, I am reminded that Sisyphus received this punishment for loving life too much, for having the gall to wheedle his way out of the underworld and then refusing to go back. The gods did not take kindly to that. But Sisyphus did not want to go under, and neither do I. I do not want to be lost in the mundane. I do not want to be submerged. And so of course that's where I am. Sisyphus and I, our pride got us where we are.

Today, with laundry all around me, I berated myself for failing yet again, for pushing the rock up the mountain only to have it fall back on me. If only the baby would take a nap, I thought, I could get through this mess, just put everything away and finish with the laundry once and for all. But then I remembered, if Nate actually did take a nap, there were a million things I needed to do that mattered more than laundry: there was a manuscript to read, several half-finished essays to write, an in-box full of e-mails to respond to, remarks to prepare for my next speaking engagement. The laundry would have to wait, I realized. And I felt guilty about that.

Some time later, I realized Nate needed changing. He is beginning to walk now, his eight-month-old chunky legs propelling him like a wobbly drunk as he grips my index fingers and staggers through the house. So we walked to his room together. The laundry piles were in their usual places, and I did my best to look right past them. I hoisted him up to the changing table, unsnapped his onesie, and leaned down to grab a diaper from the cabinet on the right of the table. Suddenly, I felt his legs whip past the hand I had left hovering next to him as I turned my gaze to the diapers for just a moment. I looked to see him spiraling, falling from the table, turning in midair like a chubby junior member of Cirque du Soleil. In an instant he was on his back, hands up around his ears, his face stunned, open-mouthed, but without a cry.

His head missed the diaper pail by centimeters, I realized as I turned to scoop him up, my body coursing with adrenaline. But why wasn't he crying? Was he unconscious? Was he hurt? No. He was surprised but completely unharmed. I realized as I picked him up from his landing pad of burpies and shirts that his two-foot fall had been cushioned—by a generous bed of dirty laundry.

Nate whimpered as I picked him up and pressed him to me, moving clothes out of the way to make room for us to sit on the futon. The guilt descended upon me like a twenty-pound baby falling off a changing table: How could I have turned my head, even for a second? How could I have been so lax? A good mother would never have let that happen, a good mother would have had the diaper prepared, no need for furtive rummaging through the cabinet, no need to peer into the jumble of wipes and baby products in search of what she needed.

But, I reminded myself, a good mother would have done her laundry. A good mother wouldn't have left a basket of dirty clothes lying around right next to the changing table, and that's surely what saved Nate from serious harm. Dirty laundry saved my baby's life, I thought to myself, laughing as Nate suddenly grabbed my hair and shrieked with excitement.

Maybe I had been reading too much into my laundry issues, making a metaphor out of a laundry pile and blaming myself for bad housekeeping and pathological resistance to change, when really what all my laundry meant was simply that I have two kids and no cleaning lady or babysitter, that I get behind sometimes and put the laundry last on my list. Maybe the subtext of having dirty laundry is nothing deeper than the fact that sometimes putting off the inevitable, hanging on to things just the way they are, can serve a purpose in some unexpected way.

Still, after I put Nate down for his nap, I arranged the diapers in the changing table cabinet. And then I picked up the dirty clothes that saved his life and put them in the wash.

A WALK IN THE PARK

Wendy Schuman

~~~~~~

As a child born and raised in New York City, Central Park was my big backyard, my daily contact with nature. The vast expanse of green in the midst of brick and concrete canyons always seemed magical to me. I loved the chestnut trees that stood like sentinels outside the playground, the fairy-tale Belvedere castle reflected in the lake, the Wollman Memorial skating rink where I learned to skate on freezing cold days and had hot chocolate after, the ornate stone bridges flanked by cherry blossoms in spring, picnics in summer on the Great Lawn. Of course I was never allowed to wander the park alone—even in the kinder, gentler 1950s, its hidden lanes and forested areas were forbidden places where bad guys lurked. Most days I stayed in the old Eighty-sixth Street playground, which had a splintery seesaw, metal swings, and a rusty slide over cracked cement. But sometimes in the company of my mother or babysitter or the "Billdave Club," an afterschool group named for the two brothers who owned it, I ventured out to see more of the park's natural beauty.

This same idyllic park was the scene of one of my worst moments—and biggest mistakes—as a mother. I'd always been very overprotective and anxious with my firstborn, Cory.

Every little thing had to be perfect, and I rarely trusted even my darling husband to take care of her properly—I was sure he'd give her expired formula or forget her sweater or have some other lapse that would result in tragedy. We were living in New York City on the Upper West Side, not far from the building where I grew up. Central Park was also the closest thing Cory had to a backyard. The Eighty-sixth Street playground had become a modernized wonder, with rubber tires, rope swings, and multilevel climbing gyms, all on a child-friendly surface of sand.

It was a soft spring day, the trees were newly green, and I decided to show Cory, then five, the natural beauty of the park. We would walk all the way across to visit Grandma on the east side of town, a trek of about two miles. Actually, this was my fantasy of what I thought would be a great experience for a mom and her city kid. In reality, Cory hated long walks and had been happy making sand pies in the playground. It took some promises of stopping en route at the carousel and getting ice cream to entice her to leave.

It started off pretty well. I pointed out some of my favorite park vistas, set off by cherry blossoms and forsythias in bloom. We crossed stone bridges and went under tunnels, making hooting sounds so we could hear the echo. We fantasized about who lived in the castle. But a five-year-old's attention span and energy are not that great, and Cory started to get bored and tired. Plus, I realized I was lost.

It seemed like the park was in some kind of repair mode. Grassy areas were fenced off to protect the newly seeded lawn, and there were detours around areas of dredging and digging. I had no idea how to find the carousel or even how to walk in a straight path toward the towering buildings on the East Side. Every turn seemed to take us into a different construction site.

My little girl was pretty miserable and asking me to carry her—but it would have been a long way to carry a weary fifty-pound child. We were pretty much stuck. There was no mode of transportation in the middle of the park, so we had to push on in one direction or the other—and catch a cab when we made it to one of the exits. We rested on a bench, and finally I asked a respectable-looking man how he thought we could walk across to the other side of town. He said we'd have to detour downtown a few blocks. He said to follow him, he could figure out the way.

One of the nice things about Central Park is that, for most of it, cars are invisible. The park is built up on a hill, a huge mound of volcanic rock through which several crosstown tunnels are cut. Cars and buses speed through these transverses, but they are below the level where park visitors walk. You can hear them but not see them. We followed our guide around some detours; I went first, then Cory.

Suddenly we found ourselves in the middle of an overpass on top of one of the tunnels where cars and buses go across town. Then I realized we were *outside* the barrier that keeps people from seeing the cars. We were about a foot from the edge of a precipice, holding on to a chicken wire fence with cars speeding back and forth about twenty feet below. If we fell, we'd fall right into oncoming traffic. I have never been so frightened in my life. All I could do was pray and say to Cory, "Honey, hold on to the fence and go sideways, like Mommy."

We walked sideways, hand over hand. It took less than a minute to get to the other side. But it was the longest minute of my life. I can't remember exactly what happened next. Did I scream at the guy who exposed us to this hazard? Did I sit down and cry and hug my daughter, grateful that she and I were both alive? My mind can't get past that long agonizing moment when I realized I had led my daughter—whom I loved more than anything and whose safety I was obsessed with—into a deathtrap. I can still hardly breathe when I think about it, and this took place more than twenty years ago. Until recently I had never even told my husband.

When I did tell him—as we were walking in the park under the billowing orange curtains of Christo's art project, The Gates—he said it was ironic that I'd been so worried about her safety with him when the only time she'd been in real danger was with me!

Of course, he was right. I don't know what lesson to draw from this, except that I wish I'd spent less time worrying about things that never happened. Fortunately, my daughter tells me she doesn't remember that spring day when I took her for a walk in the park.

Part III: Oops, I Did It Again

If you obey all the rules you miss all the fun.

—KATHARINE HEPBURN

Helene Stapinski

~~~~~~

My plan was to wean my son at one year. But after his first birthday in November, Dean got his first virus. He was so sad with his bad belly, and so skinny from vomiting, that I didn't have the heart to wean just yet. So thirteen months turned into fourteen, and fourteen into fifteen and before I knew it, Dean was a year and a half and still clamoring for my breasts. I tried to cut back, and though he took a bottle several times a day, Dean was still stuck on the booby.

The big problem was that I—along with my breasts—had to go on a book tour.

"He'll just have to go cold turkey," my husband said.

So I guiltily set out for Boston, calling in every hour or so to check on my firstborn. My husband said he was fine. He hardly missed me. Yet.

I moved on to Chicago, my breasts like giant boulders slung across my chest. I slept on my back all night, since they hurt so much. Was Dean hurting just as much? I wondered.

I felt awful, not just physically, but emotionally, for leaving Dean without his milk supply. But my husband, in call after call, reassured me Dean was a trooper, not to worry.

By the time I got to Denver, my breasts started to dry up, along with my guilt at not being home. Eric, an old friend, met me at my reading and we went out afterward to the jazz club El Chapultapec, which had been one of Jack Kerouac's favorite places. As Eric and I walked in, a quartet was wailing at the back wall. I breathed deeply of the secondhand smoke.

Though I never considered myself a real smoker, every now and then I enjoyed a cigarette or two while sitting at a bar. Pregnant, then breast-feeding, I hadn't done any smoking or real drinking in over two years. Okay, there was the occasional glass of wine with dinner, maybe a beer every now and then. But no drugs—not even echinacea when I was sick—and absolutely no hard liquor.

Pre-pregnancy, I had been a scotch drinker. I drooled now at the thought.

Eric knew the bartender from high school, so some serious drinking was about to be done. I ordered my first scotch, golden and shimmering, ice cubes glinting in the lights above the bar. The first sip, like a dose of medicine, didn't taste very good, but I knew in a minute I'd feel much better.

The scotch hit me like a pile of baby blocks. I was pleasantly buzzed. And by scotch number two, my taste buds were reacquainted with their old pal, Johnny Walker.

By the end of the night, I was so drunk that I bought a pack of cigarettes. I woke in the morning with a hangover, my body toxic from smoking half a pack of Parliaments. When I rolled over, Eric was lying next to me. Oh Christ! I thought. I've gone and slept with Eric! What kind of mother was I? But then I noticed we were both fully dressed in our stinky, smoky clothes from the night before.

Eric's eyes fluttered open, and he assured me that there had been no physical contact. I had kindly, and maternally, refused to let him drive home in such an intoxicated state. Relieved I wasn't Slut Mom of the Year, I headed out for the West Coast.

In Los Angeles, Matt, a friend of my husband's, planned on showing me the town. Matt had been a musician for years, playing bass in the ska band the Toasters, so he knew all the coolest places to go.

He took me for chicken and waffles at Roscoe's. We had a drink at the gorgeous Sky Bar at the Mondrian Hotel, with its flowering trees and its beds strewn around the pool's perimeter; I felt just like Scheherazade.

Next was the Key Club, a raunchy disco and bar filled with bottle-blondes and boob jobs. I suddenly felt old and extremely unattractive. But Matt cured that with a series of tequila shots. Since he was buddies with the bartender, every other drink was on the house.

A woman dressed in a bikini, with a holster around her waist, was offering shooters to the crowd, sitting on the lap of each male recipient and pouring shots of tequila down their throats from a long, thin glass perched between her breasts.

By midnight, I was completely hammered, and Matt, drunk off his ass. He turned to me and said, "I dare you to do a tittie shot."

"How mush will y'gimme?" I slurred. He checked his wallet.

"Forty-seven dollars," he said, grinning.

"Briggit on!" I commanded. Matt waved the bikini girl over to our booth, and before I knew it, she was sitting on my lap with her impressive cleavage in my face.

"Y' know," I slurred, looking up at her, "I'ma muvver. I lefff my bebbby at home. I shoun't be doing this. I shoun't even be here rilly."

"Ohhh," she said, sweetly, still straddling me. "How old is your baby?"

"Eighteen munts," I said, getting all teary. "You wanna see 'is piture?"

"Sure."

I leaned over and pulled my wallet from my bag, then fumbled about for his photo. "Here ee is," I said, holding the picture up to her face.

"Oh, he's so adorable," she cooed.

I looked at his little face, those big brown eyes, that button nose and told the tittie-shot girl to hit me. She gently placed the glass between her boobs, then tilted it toward my mouth. "Y'know," I said. "This is a lot like breast-feeding."

"Yeah," she laughed. "I guess it is. No one's ever mentioned that before."

I'm not sure how I got back to the hotel that night. But the next morning, I was scheduled to have brunch at the Brentwood home of Ariana Huffington, the political pundit. I considered not going, but my literary escort for the day showed up bright and early and whisked me away. I had the worst hangover of my life. Worse than those college mornings after drinking in Greenwich Village. Worse than after the high school keg parties where I had to try to walk straight through my front door under the watchful eyes of my parents.

My legs felt like noodles, my entire body hurt, and for a moment I thought I was hallucinating. In one corner was Morgan Fairchild munching on a bagel, in another corner Michael York. I was among the C-list celebrities, unable to make small talk due to my inability to stand up straight and walk across the room. I limped out into the backyard to get some fresh air, and was immediately sickened by the sight of children jumping on a trampoline. Up and down. Up and down.

"I think I have to go," I told my escort.

"What's wrong?"

"I'm hungover," I confessed.

"You should have told me," she laughed. "We can go." She paused a moment.

"But there's one thing I need you to do before we leave."

"What's that?"

"I dare you to have a go on the trampoline." I was no longer taking dares. The dare department was officially closed for the rest of the tour. For the rest of my life.

Back at my hotel, the Chateau Marmont, I lay, convalescing next to the pool. When I looked over, I noticed Iggy Pop was lying next to me on a lounge chair, his girlfriend or wife deeply tanned, with the largest boobs I had seen yet in L.A. She was practically straddling Iggy, who nearly sunk his face into her chest.

I decided then that I had had enough of L.A. and enough of my book tour.

I flew to New York the very next day, very tired. Dean looked worn out, too, strung out from going cold turkey. But there was something in the room, something I hadn't noticed before I had left. There was a bond now between Dean and my husband, shipmates abandoned by their rum-soaked captain. There were glances between them. And a love with which Dean held his daddy, which until now, had been reserved only for me, his mommy.

My first reaction was jealousy, then regret, for not being here for so long. But then my husband called him "buddy," and

Dean smiled so widely that my heart nearly cleaved in two with joy. My husband had not been lying. They had been all right without me. Without my breasts.

I scooped Dean into my lap and he put a tiny hand on my chest. He glanced down, then looked up at me sorrowfully, then shook his head, as if to say, "No go, huh?"

"All gone," I said, shrugging. He shrugged back.

I hugged him and covered him with kisses, and apologized for being away for so long. For being such a boozehound of a mother. And, like our babies do, he forgave me.

Jenny Rosenstrach

~~~~~~~~~~~~~~~~~~~~~~~~~~~~~~~~~~~~~

Before my first daughter, Phoebe, was born three years ago we made a lot of claims about parenting. With a smugness that only a childless couple can muster, we claimed we were not going to let Phoebe interfere with our annual trip abroad. We were not going to stop going out to dinner. We were not going to be slavish to nap schedules. Three years (and two kids) later, of course, you'll hear us singing the familiar defeated tune. Yes we travel, but certainly not abroad (can't deal with the time change), and yes we go out to dinner, but only if we can snag a 5:30 "dinner" reservation (I use quotes because I'm still not sure it doesn't qualify as lunch). And as far as naps go, well, put it this way: we figured out pretty quickly that we'd be idiots for voluntarily messing with a large chunk of the day that didn't involve dress-up or Dora.

But there was one outrageous pre-parenting claim that we've managed to stick with. After hearing track one of our niece's first Music Together album ("Hello Everybody, so glad to see you!") my husband, Andy, decided that he wanted as little to do as possible with the entire industry of children's music, which is defined in our house as any song that a) makes you meow, b) involves a directional element ("clap, clap, clap your hands, clap your hands together . . ."), or c) actually calls itself "Children's Music." He was even more committed to his goal after having dinner with a new dad music writer friend who had made the same resolution. He told Andy that he got through the "witching hour" evenings with his four-month-old by playing Ry Cooder and Norah Jones. "It's the same thing as candy," he explained. "If it's in the house, they'll eat it. Just don't bring the junk into the house."

This was not as easy as he thought it would be. For starters, his wife (me) grew up as a semi-celebrity in her hometown playing various lead characters in her elementary school muscials. I was Sharon in *Finian's Rainbow*, Adelaide in *Guys and Dolls*, Polly in *The Boyfriend*. There was no song that was too over-the-top for me. Kids' music seemed a natural extension for me— the perfect excuse to get back in touch with my schmaltzy roots. (My husband had declared that he was "morally opposed to musicals," early in the relationship, thereby limiting my listening access.) But even to me some of these children's music albums were criminally bad. I'd go to work with one lyric in my head and wouldn't be able to shake it until the next bad one came along. And the relentlessly educational slant annoyed me. They were continually trying to teach something—rhythm patterns, the sound of a flute versus a piccolo. Meanwhile, Phoebe was having a hard time figuring out how to transfer a drumstick from one hand to the other.

But it was impossible to keep the stuff out of the house. We had a large band of corporate forces conspiring against us—it seemed that every toy we bought played an electronica version of "Rock-a-Bye Baby," "Itsy Bitsy Spider," or "You Are My Sunshine." Her crib aquarium even had an Enya-inspired version of "Twinkle Twinkle Little Star," to our horror. But Phoebe loved it, of course. She'd drift off to sleep underneath it every night. This presented a dilemma for all of us, because even a childless person can tell you that it's downright evil to deny pleasure to your child just because of your own issues that you can't work out. So we started to make some amendments to the resolution. For instance, songs from *Sesame Street* were okay because you could make the argument that they fell under the rubric of "classic." (Even my husband had to admit that Ernie's "Honker Duckie Dinger Jamboree" had a certain charm to it.)

So yes, the kid's stuff seeps into the house, but for the most part we've had success at exposing Phoebe and now her sister, Abby, to "real" music, especially as they get older and learn how to follow the lyrics and sing along. We'd listen to our music with two sets of ears asking ourselves, "Would this make a good Phoebe song?" It was amazing to discover and in some cases rediscover the songs that did. Simon and Garfunkel's *Greatest Hits* had probably been in the CD case for ten years without airtime when Andy decided to play track 14 in the car. It was love at first listen. For three months straight we'd barely be out of the driveway before the rapid-fire requesting would begin:

"Cecilia, Daddy?"

"One second, Phoebe."

"Cecilia?"

"I'm looking for it, Sweetie."

"Cecilia?"

When the Beatles anthology was dusted off, we found that "Rocky Raccoon," "Maxwell's Silver Hammer," and "Ob-La-di, Ob-La-da" were big winners. So were songs by World Party, Cracker, Bruce Springsteen, and John Hiatt.

Of course, a song wasn't always an easy sell. Just like some parents have to put cheese on broccoli to make it appealing, we learned to become masters of spin in the music department. Before Andy played John Lennon's "Oh Yoko" he asked Phoebe, "Do you want to hear the happiest song that has ever been sung?" (How do you think a two-year-old is going to respond to that?) For a while we couldn't drive a mile without a request for "The Happy Song."

We took advantage of Phoebe's princess obsession to get her to love Loretta Lynn. The only reason she'll belt out the title track on *Van Lear Rose* is because Loretta is on the cover of the album wearing a dress that looks like Cinderella's. Loretta Lynn is known only as "The Pretty Woman" in our house.

The other important, if obvious, way to get Phoebe to love a song is to make sure that it tells a story. So it shouldn't come as a surprise that every Johnny Cash song turned out to be a hit. In "A Boy Named Sue," Phoebe giggled at the premise of the song and made us listen to the bar fight scene over and over. ("He kicked like a mule and bit like a crocodile" was her favorite line.) "Ballad of a Teenage Queen" tells the story of a movie star who moves back home to marry her first love, who works at the candy store. And the short but masterly "How High's the Water, Mama?" ("Two feet high and rising") is as good a counting song as you're going to find.

The problem with Johnny Cash, though, is that the stories he tells aren't always about animals and candy stores. One of my husband's favorites is "Cocaine Blues," a story about a drug addict who has murdered his wife and is attempting to flee to Mexico. I'm trying to convince myself that Phoebe likes it because it's set to his signature catchy riff.

But then, there was the time when I turned around to look at Phoebe in her carseat singing along to Lucinda Williams's

"Essence," a soulful, tormented yarn about a woman's addiction to drugs. With a stuffed puppy in one hand and a sippy cup in the other Phoebe mouthed the words "Shoot your love into my veins," holding the "uh" in "love" and turning "veins" into two syllables . . . just like Lucinda. That was when I realized I wasn't going to be named Mother of the Year anytime soon.

But I have to say, I'm pretty proud of the fact that Phoebe can identify Bob Dylan's voice and Abby can air guitar to "Let it Bleed." More important, by exposing them to good music, we've managed to salvage one small corner of our adult lives, which have otherwise been overrun by Nemo and Dorothy Gail from Kansas. Maybe next year we'll take them to Europe.

Kate Kelly

Years ago, I read that having pets was associated with a happy childhood. I can't remember where I read it, or if it was even a reputable source, but since getting two kittens when I was six years old is one of my happiest memories, it rings true to me. So it's a huge source of guilt that I've deprived my three boys a pet—especially because my oldest son, Jack, seven, is an avid animal lover and has been asking for a pet since he was four. He started big, begging for a dog, stepped down to a cat, a bird, a gerbil, and finally, a goldfish. No, I said to every request, knowing that, as the mother of three boys, I could not care for one more living thing, not even a goldfish.

So when my son unwrapped a "frog habitat" from a well-meaning aunt one Christmas morning, my heart sank. Naturally, Jack was thrilled, and I had to admit that the habitat looked inviting, boasting a cozy cave for the frog to hang out in, plus a pool for swimming. Given that the things had arrived, I tried to put a positive spin on the whole thing, rationalizing that this would be a good compromise, less work than a cat and not a permanent fixture in our house.

Actually, that's not entirely true. The frogs didn't actually come with the habitat. (Of course, it makes perfect sense that a live creature wouldn't be sitting in the box for months waiting to come to life . . .) Instead, Jack got a certificate entitling him to one tadpole for $4.95, or two for $9.95, which he would then nurture into frogs. Naturally, Jack wanted two and I figured, well why not. Double the fun. I sent in our check, and we waited until the weather turned warmer, as the company wouldn't be shipping our tadpoles until spring when the temperature was conducive to tadpole hatching.

I would have forgotten about our frogs-to-be, but Jack wasn't about to. As part of his second-grade homework, he had to read for twenty minutes every day after school. He would sit and pore over the directions—six pages of tiny, single-spaced type. If I had been more on the ball, I would have wondered how there could be so much to say about a couple of tadpoles, but I gave it no thought at all. We had a lot going on. We were in the midst of packing for a move to a new house that needed a lot of work. Apparently, in 1958, when the house was built, people didn't have tremendous storage needs, they didn't entertain in the casual "talk to me while I chop an onion" way we do now. They definitely didn't buy in bulk or belong to Costco.

Anyway, amid the chaos of working full time and having three children (the youngest being two), and living among boxes with nowhere to put what was unpacked, we received a small package stamped "Live Tadpoles."

The big day had come, and the timing really couldn't have been worse. But the tadpoles couldn't stay in their envelope forever—in fact, as far as Jack was concerned, they couldn't stay there for another five minutes. For the first time, I looked at the instructions that Jack had been poring over. First, we had to fill our terrarium to the two-inch line with bottled spring water, which, of course, we didn't have (we're apparently one of the few families left who finds tap water acceptable), so I zipped over to the grocery store to get the water. Then there was the elaborate process of making sure the water was the right temperature and putting the tadpoles in. We were supplied with a little packet of dried food, and we were only supposed to give one pellet at a time. The directions stressed the importance of keeping the tank clean, using a turkey baster or large medicine dropper to remove any "waste" after the tadpoles ate their pellet.

Reading ahead, I became a little alarmed. Once our tadpoles became frogs, they would have to be fed live crickets. Where were those going to come from? The directions also said that the frogs could not be let free into the wild or they would die immediately. (How long did frogs live, anyway? The directions didn't say.)

But those were problems for the future. My biggest challenge right now was where to put the tadpoles. They needed a quiet, out-of-the-way spot (no such place existed in our chaotic, crowded house), away from direct sunlight or heat. Unfortunately, the kitchen counter was the best match; unlike other potential resting spots, it was too high for my two-year-old's curious little hands, and the sunlight wasn't too intense.

For three days, all was well. Jack was careful not to overfeed; we replaced half the water, as the directions stated, with fresh water; and I religiously skimmed the tank every night for waste. Then I realized that I desperately needed the real estate upon which the tadpoles were squatting.

Hmm . . . they're Jack's tadpoles. They really belong in Jack's room, I thought to myself. So I moved them upstairs and promptly forgot about the tank.

That turned out to be a really bad decision because less than twenty-four hours later, Jack screamed from his room, "They're dead!"

I ran up, and indeed, it didn't look good. I pulled out the directions to see where we went wrong, and noted that the importance of keeping the tank clean was in caps.

Wow, one slipup, and it was over.

I tried my best to comfort Jack, saying we would send away for more tadpoles. This time, I would really be on top of it. But as far as Jack was concerned, there were no second chances.

"Why bother," he sobbed. "We'll just screw it up again."

I felt truly awful, wishing that my problem was as simple as where to get crickets. We didn't even make it to frogs. We were losers.

Now the question remained: what were we going to do with the whole mess? Nothing had ever died in our family. Well, that's not true. My husband's grandmother had died, but the kids had been too young to go to the funeral. But they were fascinated by the fact that she was buried in the ground and frequently asked exactly what happened to her body in the dirt. When I suggested we have a funeral, everyone perked up. It was a simple affair: Jack dug a hole, placed the tadpoles in it, and covered them with dirt. I hummed taps.

Four months later, we went to the pound and got not one cat, but two. I decided that nothing could be harder than keeping those tadpoles alive. There's no way around it. Having cats is work. But at least they don't die if you forget to change the litter box.

Ronnie Polaneczky

It is Saturday afternoon, and I'm sitting at tea at the Four Seasons with my three-year-old daughter.

We've never looked better. Addie's wearing a fancy dress that won't fit her after next week, probably. I'm having a good hair day.

I'm pretty cheap, so today's $45-per-person tab for eating finger sandwiches should make me wince. But I fork over four twenties and a ten with a serene smile.

It's not money.

It's shrink insurance.

If I give her enough soft-lit childhood memories, I figure, maybe my daughter won't end up on some psychiatrist's couch in twenty years, recalling in polychromatic detail my blunders as a mother.

Like last week, when I stupidly let Addie watch a lab tech poke a needle in my vein and draw blood for some routine tests.

She'll see that this is no big deal, and she'll learn not to be squeamish when she needs her own blood taken one day, I reasoned, assuming wrongly, yet again, that my child's psyche is a broad canvas whose developing landscape is under my control. What a savvy mother I am!

One minute later, I watched my kid sag, white-lipped and clammy, to her knees on the lab's shiny tiled floor, struggling to describe the totality of fainting symptoms assaulting her forty-pound body.

"Mommy," she mumbled, "I feel . . . sad . . ."

A few quick gulps of cold December air quickly revived her. But I've yet to recover from my stunning lack of judgment.

The problem, as every parent knows, is that the lessons of child-rearing are too often taught in twenty-twenty hindsight. What I learned last week is never again to let my kid watch her mother bleed. But I doubt she'll give me credit for never repeating that mistake. Instead, I'll get nailed for having made it in the first place.

My own childhood was decades ago. I'm still nailing my folks for their shortcomings.

So these days, I'm proactively courting can't-miss, way-to-go-Mom! experiences. Excursions to the zoo fall into this category, as do wearing oven mitts on my ears for a laugh, and, hopefully, attending tea today at the Four Seasons.

It's not just tea, of course. It's "Teatime in Wonderland," an annual children's sip hosted by a woman dressed like Lewis Carroll's Alice and featuring sumptuously costumed students from the Pennsylvania Ballet performing dances from *The Nutcracker,* right there on the hotel carpet.

"Teatime" is offered on only a handful of holiday Saturdays, and reservations get snatched up weeks in advance. So, in addition to being expensive, today's tea has the added cachet of being exclusive, which has attracted the privileged mother-daughter class in droves.

The dresses on some of the urchins leave me drop-jawed.

A confident-looking eight-year-old sails past me, coiffed in a French twist, wearing an ermine-trimmed frock that I'm sure cost more than my own wedding dress. Another child wears a silvery shantung silk garment accessorized by, I kid you not, a matching backpack.

My child, of course, is more beautiful than all of them in the black velvet hand-me-down my friend's daughter wore to some long-ago event. Only her purple plastic starfish necklace betrays her humble roots.

The maitre d' shows us to a cunning deuce—that's restaurant lingo for "table for two"—planted in the center of the action. A waiter fills my cup with English Breakfast, Addie's with hot cocoa.

Addie pushes her beverage aside and uses her spoon to dig, cereal-style, into its accompanying bowl of mini marshmallows. She doesn't touch the finger sandwiches, but inhales the blob of Devonshire clotted cream like it's Breyer's vanilla and eats only the green cookies on the dessert plate.

For this I've paid $45.

It all comes together, though, when we sit cross-legged on the floor with the rest of the audience and watch the ballet's bemuscled Toy Soldier leap, spin, and—slyly winking at pop culture—break-dance across the room with sublime athletic grace. Late-afternoon sunlight streams through the windows, glinting off the silver and china, making flittering jewels of each dancer, cameos of each child's upturned face. Addie absorbs the scene in entranced silence as I snap photo after photo—not of the Soldier or the Sugarplum Fairies, but of her, having a magical moment orchestrated by the Best Mother in the World.

Years from now, when she holds an opposite opinion of me, I'll beg to differ with her memories of a faulty childhood. I'll pretend not to remember things like the hypodermic incident and instead remind her of what I plan to make our annual tradition of holiday tea.

"You had a wonderful childhood," I'll tsk, absently waving a hand. And I'll have the photos to prove it.

Muffy Mead-Ferro

~~~~~~

I got the kids' school packets in the mail the other day. I had to laugh at the zeal of the school administrators, sending out stuff like cafeteria menus in the middle of the summer. Honestly, they know what the soup-of-the-day is going to be that far into the future? I hope that doesn't mean they've already prepared it. But then, I'd also gotten catalogs selling Christmas decorations in the mail, so I supposed our school wasn't getting ahead of themselves any more than the rest of the world.

Then, when I actually took the time to sit down and peruse the calendars in the packets I found that the first day of school was less than a month away.

Say what?

What in the Sam Hill happened to summer? It hit me like an icy blast of winter air that we'd neglected to *do* anything—no summer activities—and now suddenly summer itself, which back in May had seemed to stretch so long and to be so full of promise, was almost over.

Too late to start signing up for stuff now. I just hope that Belle, six, and Joe, four, won't feel like big fat losers during their first week back, because I just know that their teacher, or one of their friends, or one of their friends' parents will ask them what they did this summer and I can tell you exactly how the conversation will go.

"What'd you do this summer? Did you go to music camp?"

"No."

"Did you play on a soccer team?"

"No."

"Tennis lessons?"

"No."

"How about T-ball? Did you play T-ball?"

"What's T-ball?"

I hope this kind of back and forth won't make Belle or Joe feel bad, because the fact that we did not have a productive summer was my fault, not theirs. I'm the one who dropped the T-ball, whatever that is, and I'm just sure that every other kid and mom at our school spent the whole summer going here, there, and everywhere learning great new skills, having fantastic adventures, and expanding their little minds beyond all bounds.

And what did we do? How did we spend our precious summer days?

First of all I must admit that we slept in quite a bit. All four of us—my husband, myself, Belle, and Joe—usually ended up by about 5:00 a.m. in the same bed. But I should count Sallykraut, the dachshund, so that would be all five of us. We'd loll around tickling and bothering each other and reading the newspaper with the TV on until 8:00 or sometimes 9:00. Or sometimes—egad—10:00, on weekends.

Saturdays and Sundays we made breakfast together. One thing I will remember about this summer is that Joe and Belle decided they were capable of cooking their own meals. This never failed to produce a giant mess, and I'm sure I spent an inordinate amount of time trying to convince them that cleaning up was also part of the fun. I succeeded to the extent that I was willing to let them squirt things with Windex, but I could have cleaned the kitchen myself three times by the time they got the job done. Oh well, as far as enriching activities went, that's about the level on which we operated.

As for adventures, we visited family. My father-in-law. My mother-in-law. My father and stepmom. My grandparents. My brothers and their families. This constitutes just about as wide a variety of people and personality quirks as you'll find anywhere, let me tell you. And they visited us, too. My mother-in-law, for instance, stayed with us two times this summer, for ten days at a stretch both times, and that was a learning experience for all of us. She showed me how to make pasta e fagioli, which was new to me. And instant lemonade, which wasn't. She's quite hard of hearing and Belle and Joe had to get used to speaking a lot louder, and with better diction. That's probably worth something.

Belle and Joe learned other skills this summer, though. Belle learned how to play Crazy Eights and, to some degree, how to put on a poker face. Joe learned to ride his two-wheeler. I just hope I live long enough to see him reach another pinnacle like that one.

I did manage to sign them up for swimming lessons, and they seemed to make some real progress with their front crawl. I'm sure they would have made more if they hadn't ended up missing three of the eight classes because we drove to Cheyenne in the middle of it to visit my brother and his family. I want them to learn to swim, but I want them to know their cousins better.

What Belle and Joe mostly did this summer, though, was

play. They played inside, they played outside. Sometimes they had friends over, and every once in a while they went to somebody else's house. But most days they had only each other for entertainment. The relationship I saw developing between Belle and Joe was probably the best thing about our summer, I think. They figured out stuff for themselves to do and almost all of it was more fun if you made sure it was fun for the other person, too.

I don't mean there wasn't any fighting, because there was plenty of that, along with crying, screaming, and tattle-telling. But they got better, as the summer went on, at working their problems out without having me constantly run interference.

In any case, I've now faced the fact that this summer's a goner. Maybe next summer I'll be better organized. Maybe I'll plan ahead. Or maybe Belle or Joe or both of them will decide for themselves that they're determined to join a soccer team and if they do, there's a good chance I'll get on board. If that's how it pans out I know they'll probably have a great time, and I know I'll have a great time watching them run up and down the field in their little uniforms.

But I also know that when I look back and remember this long, slow summer, which I wish didn't have to end so soon, it'll be with a long, slow sigh.

Ayun Halliday

~~~~~~

Back in the day, I used to follow, with, I'll admit, some relish, the spectacular catfights unfolding on the discussion boards of a Web site catering to nonviolent, liberal-minded attachment-revering parents. I say parents, but in reality, these boards were frequented almost exclusively by women, many of whom lived in communities where their views on everything from cloth diapers to home schooling were considered freakish. I sometimes wondered why they didn't use their free time to research more welcoming real-life environments, instead of frittering hours away on the Internet with "friends" they knew only by screen names. Maybe they were addicted to the parenthetical cyber hugs that would start appearing within moments of any posted misfortune: a neighbor's nasty remark about a breast-feeding toddler, a squabble with ones mate, a disappointing pregnancy test, a miscarriage. (((Oh, honey! My thoughts are with you!!!!))) If the downtrodden was an especially well-known character on the site, averaging a couple of dozen posts a day, one of the witchier mamas might announce that she was going to light a candle for her that night.

I had a little snicker room because it was my good fortune to live in New York City and my addiction to the Web site did not spring from feelings of isolation. I lived in a neighborhood where women of all colors with an age spread of more than twenty years popped their titties out of leopard-print bras at the first squawk from their frequently vegetarian, not necessarily newborn young. In other words, I fit in, possibly more than I ever had in my entire life. I think a sense of belonging is imperative for first-time mothers, so that they don't lose their marbles when they're denied access to their pre-maternal identities. For me, that need was met just half a block away in the Tompkins Square playground. I put in an appearance virtually every day for two and a half years, sometimes staying for as much as four or five hours. It dawned on me that the mamas who claimed addiction to the Web site were mothers who didn't have a Tompkins Square playground of their own.

My own personal addiction to the Web site sprang from the fact that I just couldn't get over the wealth of information at my disposal. It was like having a fleet of really eager reference librarians at my beck and call twenty-four hours a day! "Screw cyber hugs," I typed. "Who wants to tell me how to get three years' worth of baked-on grease out of my oven without giving my one-year-old irreversible brain damage?"

"LOL!" came a near-instant reply "Put a pan of ammonia on baking rack and let sit 24 Hrs then sponge that gunk right off."

"Thanks, Echinacea76," I hammered politely back, already half an hour late getting dinner started. "Hey, what the f-in' h-e-double-hockey-sticks does LOL mean?"

"LOL!!! You crack me up! Before I forget, don't turn your oven on while ammonia's in there or you'll explode. (LOL)"

I cracked her up! And now I knew how to clean my oven! Getting a laugh was even more seductive than getting free advice. I refined my comedic patter as I trolled for information on how to deal with lice, mildewed tub toys, and wool sweaters shrunk three sizes by the Laundromat's dryer. And as a matter of style, I refused to abbreviate or even use the phrase "laughing out loud," once I figured out what it meant. You can't be the jester if you behave like a member of the court.

The Web site's discussion forum was divided into some twenty or so categories. My most frequent visits were to Miscellaneous, where I posted my sidesplitting domestic inquiries, and Entertainment, where I pimped the zine I had recently started publishing. I put in an occasional appearance at Sex. If I was really procrastinating, I might rummage around in Travel to reminisce about pre-motherhood global adventures and dispense some advice of my own.

The categories that addressed the nitty-gritty of childrearing held less interest for me. I got my fill of that, both good and bad, every day on the playground. The last thing I wanted to hear when I came home was a bunch of those cute nicknames toddlers invent for their mothers' breasts. Even in a non–face-to-face forum, I could sense the competitive edge, each poster painfully invested in having her child's word perceived to be the most adorable of the lot. Neither was I burning to see jpegs of other peoples' kids, especially since I lacked the technical mastery needed to post some of my own. Contrasting various strollers, high chairs, car seats, Boppi pillows, and organic rice cereals was a snore. Don't these hens have anything better to do with their time, I thought, before I reminded myself that I might be clucking a different tune myself if I didn't have so many real live mother friends with whom to compare notes.

Not that the women dishing out cyber hugs weren't made out of meat, it's just . . . I don't know, mama-centric topics that struck me as stimulating enough in the shadow of the jungle gym seemed dead dull in a medium so beautifully suited to amateur pornography and the near-psychotic ramblings of obsessive fans.

Skirting the categories that were the boards' raison d'etre kept me out of the loop somewhat. I'd be over in Miscellaneous, agitating for someone to come forward in order to repost the homemade bath-bomb recipe she'd shared the previous Christmas, completely unaware that ten days earlier, her son had been rushed to the emergency room, where he nearly died of meningitis. The Toddler Talk regulars, on the other hand, had been monitoring the situation closely since it began, embracing every update with a veritable storm of parentheses and lit candles. Some of them came through with more tangibly thoughtful expressions of concern like running the details of the diagnosis past a family member who was a pediatric attending at Cedars Sinai or arranging for a meal to be delivered to the hospital.

Even taking into account the medical or romantic crisises that didn't necessarily show up on my shuck-and-jiving radar screen, I probably would have persisted in my belief that everything was hunky-dory had someone not cross-posted in every category an announcement that a certain user had been banned from the community. The screen name Udderlywonderful meant nothing to me until she was given the boot for saying something "unforgivable," "insensitive," "racist," and "stupid" to MamaDaffodil, a hard-core user with thousands of posts to her name. Sounded juicy! I spent hours looking for the original thread, but came up with zilch, even after sifting through the dregs of Mamas of Teens, not surprisingly the least active category on the board. I later learned that a volunteer moderator had expunged all evidence. This deletion did not lay the matter to rest by any means. Dozens lined up to pledge their allegiance to the traumatized MamaDaffodil, to shower her with cyber hugs, to express their outrage that such a thing could have happened in our "safe" community and to beg everyone to meditate upon this horrible moment in the site's history so that we could move past it and hopefully learn something. The mind reeled imagining what the villainous Udderlywonderful might have said to move others to the kind of rhetoric more appropriately applied to the Holocaust and other genocides of the twentieth century. Was it possible that she'd made an ill-tempered remark because her two-year-old had been driving her crazy all day, grappling to get at her boobs in the post office and staging a truly operatic tantrum in the supermarket cereal aisle? A charge of racism had been leveled against her, but in my book, that's not one to accept immediately or on face value alone. It was weird, too, because I'd seen jpegs of the ubiquitous Daffodil and her family and they were all blue-eyed blonds. Was the charge then actually one of reverse racism? Nah, couldn't be. No one on the site would have been so insensitive as to eject one of the few African-American, Latina, or Asian users for calling a member of the majority a honky or a cracker. Actually, I'd noticed that the frequent claims of identification made by members of the site's liberal white majority tended to drive the handful of Mothers of Color—who had a category unto themselves—absolutely barking mad. They were also embroiled in an internal stand-off as to whether white mamas of interracial children should be considered Mothers of Color themselves. As a white woman given to conflict avoidance and having people like me, I never posted in Mothers of Color, but I'd read its threads often enough to know that had some real racial slur been uttered, there were six or seven regulars who would have been all over it, without mincing words. Strangely, the Udderlywonderful affair didn't seem to register at all over there. Perhaps the Mothers of Color were traveling to Breastfeeding or Pregnancy to express their indignation, because it was hot news on every other part of the board.

I noticed that the outpouring was not limited to those who had been lucky enough to witness the original train wreck. Plenty of posters prefaced their remarks by saying that they didn't know what Udderlywonderful had said, but that they couldn't believe she had been so insensitive. Whoever said that it takes a lot of sheep to make a revolution was onto something.

I wish I could say that I had come forward with a Portia-like appeal to mercy and reason, but no way was the beloved jester who had made those now clamoring for cyber-blood LOL in happier days going to stick her neck out for a new user who was gone for good. Whoever Udderlywonderful was, she'd written a tearful farewell upon learning of her exile, in which she spoke of how much the community had meant to her and how she would really miss some of the "good friends" she'd made there and concluded by telling all the expectant mothers that she'd be lighting a candle for each of them to have a beautiful birth. One of the community members had thoughtfully cut and pasted this final missive into one of the denouncement threads, so that others could rip it to shreds.

Dang, how I wish I'd hopped in to ask if maybe this was all just a tempest in a teapot. Maybe MamaDaffodil had been the one having a crap day. Was it possible that she had overreacted to something that had been intended as a joke? Maybe she'd posted yet another photo of her youngest child covered in spaghetti and Udderlywonderful, speaking for all of us, had replied "For the zillionth time, he's adorable, all right? Can we give it a rest?" And MamaDaffodil, whose twins wouldn't stop shrieking that her vegan ratatouille looked like diarrhea had lashed back with a bit more viciousness than the situation warranted. As someone quite intimate with the frustrations of raising small children in a loving, nonviolent manner, I could see it happening.

But I couldn't see it happening on Tompkins Square playground. Why? Because we knew each other's real names. Because our kids had to share the same slides and swings. Because the importance of facial expression and tone of voice were not lost in translation, the way they are on the Internet. Because we knew how awkward and unpleasant tomorrow's visit to the playground would be if tempers were allowed to flare today. Because there was little likelihood that a multitude of supporters would fling themselves onto the pig pile over an unsubstantiated grievance. Because it's presumptuous to think you can banish fellow citizens from a location you don't own, unless they're sex offenders or drug dealers or something. Because politeness remains a virtue, even when you're itching to tear someone a new asshole for some snotty remark she's made. Because community is so important during the isolating early years of motherhood, it would be foolish to start blowing holes in it for no good reason.

Hole blowing. That pretty much sums up what led to the demise of an online parenting community, which was founded on the admirable ideals of information sharing and mutual support. The Udderlywonderful outcome set a precedent whereby pretty much everyone seemed to think it was her responsibility to rout out narrow-mindedness, intolerance, homophobia, sizeism, conservatism, or any sentiment that could be construed as anti, except when it had been applied to vaccines, TV, fast food, mothers-in-law, or other approved evils. In other words, to blow it out their holes. And the nature of the community shifted from a place where you could bitch about stretch marks, soccer mom stereotypes, and the baby that wakes up screaming just when you're about to have sex for the first time in months into a place where behaving self-righteously masqueraded as being right, which, I'll be the first to admit, is a maternal need almost as great as the need for community. A place where bullies declared that g's were p's and q's were u's and those judged guilty of uttering them were given a good thrashing before they were tossed out on their ears. A place where the sheep scrambled to back the wolf so they wouldn't be next on the menu. But for the civility of every social interaction I witnessed and participated in on my actual playground, I'd be tempted to apply the old saw, "the law of the playground," to the bad behavior that became the order of the day on the Web site for mindful, nonviolent, attachment-revering parents (actually just mothers). Can they be said to have been acting like children, when they aspired to raise children who would respect others' cultures, their own bodies, animals, the earth, and the First Amendment? Should silly screen names really have such a degree of magical dress-up power that Peanutbutterfly feels it's her right, nay, responsibility to excoriate Smurfgirl1968, even though Julie would never speak that way to Karen's face, especially when she doesn't know what that face looks like. It goes without saying that not one of these mothers would have permitted anyone to treat their children so obnoxiously.

Finally, the exasperated volunteer moderators shut the site

down after repeated orders to play nice failed to have any effect. When they learned that the site was going belly-up at midnight, a lot of mothers mourned the loss of this community, even as they scrambled to regroup elsewhere in cyberspace. I decided to spend even more time in the playground. It seemed there was a lot to be gained from a little fresh air.

Part IV: So Much Gray

Most mothers are instinctive philosophers.
— HARRIET BEECHER STOWE

ODE TO GRAY

Lu Hanessian

~~~~~~

Somewhere between the delivery room and my son's front tooth wriggling out last week, I figured out that intuition is something we're born with, learn to suppress throughout childhood, reject by adolescence, and then, after flailing in the open seas of adulthood, attempt to retrieve. But by then, with no compass to locate its whereabouts, how do we recognize it? Often, we hire someone, an intuitive other, to track it down for us. And then *poof*, it's gone. Scared off by barking dogs.

My own intuition had long been in shackles by the time I brought home my precious newborn for whom popular opinion was not at all popular. He defied baby book logic, hissed at theories and parental convenience, at black and white answers. He asked me to quit searching out there, to come inside from the cold, and start doubting myself for real. His six-pound, nine-ounce body craved touch while his mind whirred relentlessly. I stood at the crossroads of resistance and surrender, engorged and entranced, feeling both undaunted and defeated by my new role as Mother. I stared at the man-child, his intuition intact. He had no words, nowhere to go, and yet he knew how to suckle, knew his own needs, for crying out loud—which he did a lot. Then, after a good crying jag in my arms, he was calm, having returned himself to equilibrium, finding his peace when I was still in pursuit of my own.

Put him down, the chorus chanted. *Show him who's boss . . .*

My maternal gut churned. My own voice was faint but audible. What did I really believe? What does a person need to feel in order to birth a bona fide conviction? What compels someone to choose one path, one belief, one action, over another? My baby, with all his sensitivities to light, sound, crowds, strollers, cars, vacuums, lawnmowers, blenders, stethoscopes, strangers tickling his wattle, baths, diaper changes, gas, and anything that initially resembled but was not in fact a breast, invited me into the gray zone to make myself at home. Then, he belched hard, which, for a new mother, was a gift. *At last*, I thought, *a definitive answer*. Gas was such a gray area in those early months. So was colic. And sleeping the night.

Shades of black and white. Was there ever such a thing as a hard fact? The math of motherhood doesn't add up that way. Not only is there *so much* gray, but so many kinds of it. There's the gray haze of sameness, a perceptual illusion that makes us think nothing's changing. The pallid gray vulnerability of sleep deprivation. The gray by-product of maternal vigilance in a world of impossible safeguards. That zero-gravity gray where our kids are forever untethered and we can't do a damn thing about it. The familiar bleached-out gray of pathological fence-sitting. *What should I do? What can I do?* There's the salty sea gray of possibility or the sooty gray of avoidance. The holding-cell gray, a place where fears and hypotheticals bully each other into paralysis, our dread consuming our courage. The gray fog of self-doubt, living in the retrospect of the moment—the future history of the present. *Did I do the right thing? Will I have done the right thing?* The dusty gravel of ambivalent choices, wondering always if the road taken is the better one. And, of course, the airless gray shroud that comes from looking over your shoulder comparing yourself to every other mother and your children to theirs.

Pregnant with my first child, the ambiguity was about gender, eye color, a middle name, white eyelet or yellow for the bassinet, a new life order, a different configuration of marriage. Across the threshold, pangs of grown-up adolescent insecurities. Feeble motions to camouflage. The pretense of confident mothering, making it look like we're in control, like we know how it all turns out, like the way it turns out vindicates us and justifies our choices, like we're entirely convinced of those choices when we're making them.

The boy was about to teach me a thing or two about love and fear and how the two can only coexist for so long before all hell breaks loose. Somehow, intuition has a radar for defense, for the stalemate of resistance, and tends to burrow down, down, down to hibernate for all time, until we summon it. And even then, it hedges, waiting for us to choose. It can wait forever. It might be tempted to reemerge, even through a lingering ambivalence, if one can, say, stop gripping the armrests of an airplane seat during unexpected turbulence, thinking that, maybe, if one squeezed hard enough, the plane will actually stop bouncing around.

I look down from the window as we approach Newark airport after a short trip down south, staring at a waffle grid of streets and telephone lines through thin cloud, rows of gray brick houses standing side by side like tombstones. I'm not particularly depressed, just tired.

Six years after newborn colic, I wrestle with my intuitive

demons in the halls of my kindergartener's school, the place he likes to call "jail."

"The teacher is so *mean* to me," he laments, bewildered. I file this statement through my internal tracking system, screening its contents, and giving it a polygraph before I unearth its subtext using my maternal Geiger counter.

"When we sit on the circle for the story, I can't see the book, so I change positions to get closer. And she says, *Stop squirming or I'll have you sit in the blue chair.*" He takes on her low staccato voice, his face void of emotion.

"What's the blue chair?"

"It's a chair she makes me sit in to punish me," he says, "and when I sit in it, my heart pounds so fast it feels like it's about to explode! She's like . . . ten thousand pirates trying to steal my lungs, bones, and body." Read: I can't breathe or move in there.

"I gave him *six* chances to write the sentence," says the fifty-something teacher as we stand in the doorway of the classroom, her pointer finger punctuating the number. "He needs a shadow in the class," she concludes after a week, which, to him, would be more like a *hundred* thousand pirates.

"A shadow?" I ask.

"I don't have time to work with him," she reasons. "I have seventeen others."

My six-year-old self-motivated kid who loves to learn now hates school. *What should I do? What can I do?* I meet with the principal, who later asks to visit with my son alone for a few minutes. When I join them, my son looks pale and frightened, his eyes blinking back tears. The principal turns to me and says, "I had him all pumped up to come back, and then you walked in and he changed. I think he's trying to control you."

What can a mother do at a moment like this but stand in a kind of numb awe? I see her across a chasm, a tiny figurehead in a navy suit, her words hanging over the divide in a dense cloud of projections and protocol. My son and I politely dismiss ourselves.

Weeks later, in the school conference room, her seven-person school committee unanimously recommends that the boy most of them have never met should be tested and classified by their child-study team. I stare at them as they all nod collusively, and want to scream like Al Pacino. *You're out of order! This whole court is out of order!* I refrain. Maybe they really do want to help us. Maybe I am too suspicious. Maybe this isn't a covert strategy to control my son and make *him* the problem. Maybe I should home school him.

Four days pass, during which time I consume four Toblerone chocolate bars and forget to exhale. I stare at my hands, dry and cracked like a lumberjack's, and I pray. Not a *Please make this work* prayer, but a humble request for more information. What if this isn't supposed to work out? I mean, maybe this is supposed to be a bad fit for a good reason. I pray for my intuitive heart to point me, him, in the right direction.

My son and I are sitting in our van at a red light when I spot a mammoth Wal-Mart sign with huge capital letters.

"What does that blue sign say, the one with the big white letters?" I ask.

"Wal," he starts, "Ma . . ." He pauses. "Maaaaa . . ." he hangs on the vowel. "Matarsess!" he finally blurts like a game show contestant. I suddenly notice that right underneath the word *mart*, in small lowercase yellow letters, it says, *We sell for less.*

The light turns green, and the car behind me honks two blasts and leans on the second one.

"It's called convergence insufficiency," says the pediatric optometrist. "It's an eye-teaming problem, highly treatable with vision therapy a couple of times a week for a few months. He is working so hard to keep his left eye seeing with the right one. It's extremely exhausting, distracting, and requires an enormous amount of his energy, attention, and concentration."

"Would this affect his behavior and work in a classroom?" I ask rhetorically, feeling like a mother detective cracking a case wide open.

"Without a doubt," he says. "I'd like to have teachers see through his eyes for just one hour, right on the very *edge* of double vision, and find out how they would feel and what they'd do."

I pass along the information to the new kindergarten teacher. At my request, the principal had reluctantly allowed my son to switch classrooms, a rare decision in her halls. We're taking it day by day. Gray by gray.

"He'll never have the perfect teacher," people say, the same people who wondered when I'd wean, whether he was sleeping the night, when I'd be going back to work. "You're right," I say, knowing that this has everything to do with imperfection. Accidental clues, flawed perceptions, unfounded fears, struggles that lead us invariably to the right questions. Somewhere along the way, we make a trail, the stones becoming our answers only after we've laid them down.

I don't know where the path leads or what things look like around the bend. I only know that, right now, between home and the classroom, and some occupational and vision therapy and karate and swimming and kitchen science experiments and backyard musicals with friends and inventions that are born of a child's intuitive need to be himself, he is thriving.

He can see better. I can see better. The rest is gray. As it should be.

Mary Elizabeth Williams

I knew I wasn't doing a bang-up job feeding my kid before she was even born.

I'd been taking prenatal vitamins and drinking calcium-fortified orange juice, but I also laughed in horror when I picked up a pregnancy guide that suggested whole wheat oatmeal cookies (ha!) as a once-a-month (ha! ha! HA!) treat. The turning point was when I took a sample class from a natural childbirth instructor, and she asked us all to write down everything we'd eaten that day. I didn't get any extra credit for honesty when I handed in my sheet—I had cheerfully hoovered a slice of pepperoni pizza and hot fudge sundae minutes before the class commenced. The teacher looked at the page as if I'd confessed to washing down my crack with a forty of malt liquor. "You know," she said, "everything that goes into you goes into your baby. But it's okay," she added brightly, "you can do better tomorrow." I hung my cured meat– and cheese-loving head in shame, and five years later, I'm still trying for that better tomorrow.

You start out with good intentions. You watch a baby open her rosebud mouth to you, and the delight and trust on her face are so pure it makes you want to cry. When I recently bought my second daughter her first solid food, I trotted to the natural food store and picked out a box of organic brown rice cereal. Then I gave the four-year-old a handful of M&Ms. I may not be some Jerry Springer–ready trailer trash mom filling her infant's bottles with Coke, but I've got a job, two kids, and three meals a day plus snacks to fall short on, and heaven knows I do.

I have a hard enough time trying to feed myself right, but now I have to be not just the chief house chef but a decent role model. It's exhausting. I know I can't expect my daughters to sit down and eat square meals at regular intervals if I'm grabbing a bag of Tostitos and calling it lunch. They won't learn to read nutrition labels if I don't drag them to the supermarket and have them watch me do the same. They won't someday be able to feed themselves if I don't invite them into the kitchen to cook. And they won't believe that being a woman doesn't automatically mean being forever on a diet unless they're raised by one who isn't herself. Yet here I sit, quietly craving a diet Snapple and wishing to God we'll get takeout for dinner tonight.

I watch my older daughter on the playground, and I catch my breath a little every time a friend offers her some high-fructose treat. Do I have her best interests at heart if I say she can't have it, or is it better to let her, and assume it's a valuable lesson in sharing? I can pull out any of my dozens of cookbooks and make fabulous homemade macaroni and cheese for dinner, knowing damn well it'll be greeted with disappointment, or shrug as I rip open the blue box of Kraft. I struggle for an answer when she asks, "How many more carrots do I have to have before I can eat dessert?" And I kick myself when I let the baby have the sweetened applesauce when it's the only thing at the store and we're far from home.

I used to be able to control every morsel that went into

my elder daughter's mouth, as I do now with the baby. I nursed her, and then I fed her organic baby food and pureed fresh fruits and vegetables for her. And I still managed to feel inadequate—was all that fruit creating an overdeveloped sweet tooth? Was I sending her down the road to white flour addiction by letting her teethe on a bagel? Cheerios? Loaded with salt! Yogurt? A sugar bonanza! Those playground staples, Goldfish and Teddy Grahams? Don't even ask. Then one day, at another child's first birthday party, she snatched a fistful of chocolate cake off the table and shoved it greedily into her little mouth. It was the happiest I think she'd ever looked. And it taught me something, something I'd heard long ago in Catholic school but never fully understood until then. We don't have to be of the world, but we do have to live in the world. Chocolate cake happens, and it's not a tragedy when it does.

The thing about food is, it isn't just food. What's obvious from the way my baby nuzzles contentedly on my breast, taking not just milk but love and comfort and security, becomes so much more tangled up the minute a child first pries herself off mom and toddles over to a bowl of Veggie Booty. I want to raise my kids to be healthy, strong women who get their recommended daily allowances of vitamins and minerals. I want them to be highly skeptical of at least half the chemically altered, nutritionally vacant stuff at the supermarket, no matter how alluring and brightly colored it may be. But I also want to give them joy, and sometimes joy is a candy-coated milk chocolate that melts in your mouth, not your hand.

It's not sufficient for me to raise them to eat healthy food. I have to figure out, every damn day, how to raise them to have a healthy relationship with food—which, paradoxically, means making room in our lives for unhealthy food. While I can feel satisfied that my children have never had fast food or soda, I want to feel equally okay when the inevitable moment comes that they do. They're girls, and it's going to be different for them. Someday, probably soon, someone will tell them about going low carb or high protein or counting calories. And soon after they may lose their gift for devouring second helpings with unself-conscious enthusiasm, they may stop loving their beautiful bellies and their round angel faces as much as they do now. I cringe every time I lazily let my preschooler order a hot dog for dinner, but if the alternative is making her feel there's something catastrophic about it, I'll live with the guilt. I'll take inspiration from my husband, a man whose relationship with vegetables is ambivalent at best, and simply serve up the fries with a side of broccoli, the ice cream with a few strawberries. And the funny thing is, left to their own devices, they actually eat both with gusto, growing and thriving on a mix of healthy meals and occasional flat-out crap.

I don't want them looking for happiness in a box of Ding Dongs, but I really don't want them growing up under a mother who neurotically rations out their food or greets their pleasure in something from the ice cream truck with a disapproving eye. All I can do is feed them lovingly, talk to them honestly, and hope they listen. That, after all, is what the dinner table was made for, even when there's pizza on it.

Louise Kennedy

~~~~~~

"Where is your kid going to camp?" It's such a simple question, but I have come to believe—even with only one summer under my belt—that how you answer that question is not simple at all.

For example, there are the mothers who research the various day camps in their area as if their children were applying to college. They get brochures, they seek recommendations from friends, they visit ten places. Let me state right up front that I am not one of those mothers.

I asked around a little, and I gathered that we had essentially two local options in our price range: Fastidious Acres and Camp Muddimuck. Fastidious Acres, I was assured, provided a full range of enrichment activities, including stimulating crafts in an air-conditioned facility, nutritious yet toothsome lunches, and a choice of two swimming pools for carefully supervised water-safety instruction. We went with Muddimuck.

"They come home filthy and exhausted" was what a friend had told me about this camp, and, perverse as it may seem, that sounded like just the right kind of place for my rambunctious son. I bought two pairs of cheap sneakers—on the sound advice of that same friend, who warned me that muddy shoes can take a full day to dry out—and a gallon of sunscreen, loaded a backpack with water bottles and bathing suits, and packed my own darn lunch.

On the eve of the first day, I surveyed our supplies—and the eager little kindergartner who would be hauling them onto the camp bus at 8:24 sharp—and congratulated myself on having chosen a real, down-to-earth, unfussy place for C.J. to spend his summer days. Not for us the hyperprotective, coddled atmosphere of some fancy-pants establishment. If he was going to camp, by golly, he was going to *camp*.

At 8:35 the next morning, when a jam-packed bus finally hove into view, I had my first pangs of misgiving. There were not even enough seats for all the campers. My son, who had never been on a school bus in his life, would take his first ride standing up. Unacceptable—not to mention, I'm guessing, illegal. The counselors (gee, they looked so much younger than they had at the open house the week before) raised their eyebrows when the other parents and I objected, but they had to agree that the riders should all be sitting down. So they jammed the kids in closer together, three or even four to a seat, and promised that they'd speak to the scheduler about adding another bus to the route. Then off they went.

I fretted as the bus drove out of sight, and I fretted through the rest of that day until I met the bus at pickup time. Then C.J. bounced off—looking, as promised, both filthy and exhausted—and declared that he'd had a great day. "We hunted for frogs!" he exclaimed, and he displayed the muddy fingernails to prove it. Frogs and mud, I thought—isn't that what camp is all about?

So I relaxed. But then came the wasps. A whole nest of them, in fact—and, C.J. reported with awe, another camper had stepped right into the nest. Her legs were covered with stings.

Hmm. Well, on the other hand, that's nature, right? When you're in the woods, there are going to be wasps.

And poison ivy. But did there have to be quite so much of it? And wasn't there something they could do about getting it out of the sandy area that was reserved for a favorite game? Or maybe they could move the game?

But he loved it. Filthier and filthier, more and more exhausted, C.J. fell ever deeper under Muddimuck's spell. He made new friends and cemented bonds with the ones he'd known from school. He told us camp jokes. He learned to swim.

And then he got off the bus one afternoon and told us that he had bumped his head on a wall when a friend pushed him too hard on a cart; when I asked where the counselors were at the time, he said they'd been too busy chatting to notice. Oh, and not one but two people had gone to the emergency room that day. A camper had broken her finger and a counselor had broken his leg.

I was furious about the cart. And a broken leg sounded a little more serious than poison ivy. And a counselor? Weren't they the ones who were supposed to keep my kid safe, not get into danger themselves?

In a rush, all my earlier misgivings came pouring back, and I saw the situation for what it was. In my snobbish, earthier-than-thou desire to keep my kid away from the fancy-pantsers, I had blithely signed him up for what was, clearly, a deathtrap. Muddimuck's laid-back atmosphere was really a tragedy waiting to happen. My insouciance was actually negligence. I was not a free spirit; I was just a terrible mother.

I called the camp director to get the full story on the cart incident and to ask how a counselor could have been injured. It didn't help my mood that I didn't hear back from her for two days. But, still, I kept putting C.J. on the bus. (In case you needed more proof of my negligence.) And, still, he kept getting off it, filthy but safe.

Finally I heard from the director. She apologized for the apparent lack of supervision when the campers were playing with a "cart," but it turned out to be a little wooden scooting thing that could barely get above walking speed, and she'd warned the counselors to pay more attention. And the broken leg? Actually a torn tendon, the result of overuse—this counselor was an athlete who had been overtraining, and when he was walking across a field, he put his foot down funny and something just snapped.

I felt sorry for him, but also relieved. No one could blame the camp for that injury. And, I quickly realized, what I really meant was that no one could blame me. I had not chosen a terrible camp. I had not placed my child in terrible danger. I was not a terrible mother.

Or was I? Was my willingness to accept the director's explanations just one more proof of my failure to take proper care? Sure, C.J. got through the summer safe and happy—but do I really get any credit for that? Or was it just dumb luck?

Here's what I've decided: I don't know. I don't know if I am right to want him to have an authentic, messy, maybe riskier experience than his friends at Fastidious Acres—who, by the way, seemed to love their camp, too—or if I am just finding ways to justify my own preferences for the rough-and-tumble over the neatly manicured, the spontaneous over the hypermanaged, the (to revert to my own childhood for a moment) hippie over the prep.

But I do know, as I think more deeply about the choices my husband and I have made for our child, that Camp Muddimuck isn't an aberration. C.J. went to a funky but loving preschool. We let him stay up too late because he loves to read—and he's reading comic books, not classics. He gets weird leftovers instead of packaged convenience foods in his lunchbox. He seems happy with all of this because, it turns out, like his parents he prefers things a little messy.

And, next summer, he's going back to Muddimuck.

Shana Aborn

Open any parenting magazine, and you're sure to find an article with a title like "Is Your Home a Hazard?" Typically, the story features safety experts exploring a house and pointing out the hundreds of ways a child could hurt himself in every room if given the opportunity. I hate reading those articles, knowing that my apartment resembles all the "before" pictures. Our furniture has sharp corners and drawers without childproof latches. Book galleys and manuscripts are stacked in precarious piles all around the computer desk; sharp pens and pencils litter my husband's drawing table. There are no locks on the toilet, refrigerator, or DVD player. It's one big kiddie obstacle course. If one of those experts ever dropped by and realized that a two-year-old lived here, she'd weep.

It's not that my husband and I don't care about our son's safety. It's just that it's so much harder for parents today to protect their children. Back in the dawn of time, the only preventive measures Cave Mom had to take were keeping the kids away from the fire, the pointy arrowheads, and the occasional sabertooth tiger. Pioneer mothers had to contend with typhoid, lack of food, and hypothermia; they didn't worry too much about their babies getting a splinter from the wall of the log cabin. My own mother and her peers treated us kids as new-comers to the world they inhabited. They guided us around their habitat as best they could, trusting to their own instincts, a few basic safety warnings and a little luck to keep us from in-juring ourselves too badly.

But common sense isn't enough anymore. We've become a child-centric society that demands that our living space be re-arranged to fit the needs of our wee ones. To be considered suc-cessful, we have to cram our homes with furniture, electronics, and breakables—and to be considered responsible parents, we have to keep our children from touching any of them.

The list of safety measures new parents are expected to take is mind-boggling. Entire wings of baby stores are devoted to devices that block, lock, restrict, restrain, plug up, shut down, wrap around, protect, and prevent. (None of which come cheap, I might add.) If you don't want to be branded an unfit mom, you'd better make sure your house is more padded than a box of crystal stemware. It's hard to judge which products are must-haves and which you can omit without putting your child in harm's way. Is it okay not to buy a pad for the inner door-jamb that protects against finger-pinching if you already have a cover on the knob that keeps the kids from opening the door in the first place?

That's just a small part of our obsession with children's well-being. Every day brings a new expert warning about issues like infants' crib safety (no stuffed toys or tummy-down sleeping), TV watching (not at all before age two and strictly limited thereafter), and food (the list of potential allergens alone is an inch thick). To me, the holidays don't really start until the eleven o'clock news starts airing the "Kids' Holiday Hazard" reports on unsafe toys, flammable trees, and eggnog poisoning. But that's another story.

In my defense, I have to say that we do try to protect Daniel from the most obvious dangers. We keep cleaners and heavy pots in locked cabinets, open outlets plugged, latches on the windows, a safety knob on the bathroom door, smoke and carbon monoxide detectors in their proper places. Our bureau and junk drawers are two-handed jobs that are tough enough for an adult to open, much less a toddler. But that's about as far as we've gone. We tried putting those thick pads on the tables with the sharpest corners. The double-sided tape came unstuck after a couple of weeks, the pads fell to the floor, and Daniel started nibbling on them. Sure, I worry that our place doesn't resemble the "after" pictures in the safety articles, and sometimes it nags at me that I might not be doing enough. On the other hand, bubble-wrapping and double-locking all our belongings might lead to a false sense of security. Knowing that there are some hazards around the house makes me keenly aware that I have to be alert during Daniel's every waking moment.

Call us lucky, but so far Daniel hasn't suffered too badly from his parents' laxity. It helps that he isn't one of those kids who has to climb on every bookcase or open every cabinet. When he does approach something potentially ouchy, a "no, no" usually does the job; if not, we whisk him out of harm's way. His most heart-stopping injury in his short life has been a cut above his eye when he tripped and fell face-first onto a videotape box. A Disney video, no less. *The Lion King*. Which he's not allowed to watch yet because we're afraid he might be upset by Mufasa's death. A few years ago, my husband and I went to see *Sleepy Hollow,* a thriller featuring multiple murders and the ghoulish Headless Horseman. We sat directly behind a family with three children, all of them younger than eight. One little boy kept whimpering, "It's not real, Daddy, right? Right?" Which scar will linger longer—the one on Daniel's face or the one on that boy's psyche?

We all have our definitions of danger, and I'm not the only mother who plays fast-and-loose with her child's well-being. At our neighborhood playground, moms nonchalantly puff cigarettes over their infants' strollers. They give their two-year-olds pocketfuls of miniature cars meant for much older children ("Choking Hazard: Small Parts"). I know a couple of women who use only nontoxic household cleaners because they firmly believe the chemical-laden ones will make their children cancer prone. But I'd be willing to bet that their kids go to McDonald's just as often as anyone else's, even though the cheeseburgers and fries will probably damage their bodies more quickly than bleach residue on the kitchen floor would. Being a mom means making tradeoffs.

I also take comfort in knowing that I'm not the only mother whose home isn't totally latched and padded. "The world isn't going to be childproofed for my kids," a friend of mine once said. "I figured it would be easier to teach them not to touch anything without permission." My mother-in-law has upheld the same philosophy through four children, all of whom made it to adulthood without impaling themselves on the furniture or mangling a finger in a door. When the grandkids come to visit, she stows the medicines and Mr. Clean well out of reach and lets the toddlers have the run of the house under her practiced eye.

So when Daniel comes running to me in years to come with

a bumped head or a skinned knee, my heart will ache to see him crying and bruised. I'll feel guilty as hell wondering if I could have prevented it, even if I couldn't. But I know that he'll also be learning a lesson in caution and practicing for the bigger bumps of life that won't be conveniently wrapped in foam rubber—the ones from which not even the most loving and conscientious mother can protect him.

Trish Dalton

My daughter turned four today. Indicative of her newly sanc-
tioned maturity, she actually looked hurt, real deep down hurt,
when I told her I wouldn't be at her day care for cupcakes and
singing at snack time. It isn't that I forgot her special day—I
was up until midnight organizing loot bags and hand placing
colored sprinkles on pink frosted cupcakes. But I had a busy
day ahead of me. In a busy week. In a busy season. I couldn't
justify leaving work at noon to get a train to get the car to
drive to the day-care center in the nick of time to sing "Happy
Birthday."

I had thrown a princess party for her and her friends the
previous Sunday. She was celebrating with her grandmother,
aunts, uncles, and cousins on the following Sunday. We would
have special dinner and cake for her at home on her birthday
night. She was getting plenty of Happy Birthday attention.
And because she is such a good sport, I knew she would be
okay with me missing the day-care birthday party.

Does this sound defensive? I feel defensive. I know I can't
feel guilty. Guilt is merely our cover for doing what we want
to do anyway. Somehow we feel less selfish if we cloak our
choices in guilt. We all have our roles to play. I've been doing a

good job playing mine—working mother with two small children. I mostly enjoy my job, feel lots of pressure on the work and home fronts, do my best to juggle everything, and occasionally wonder if it is all worth it. Boogies smeared on my suede jacket aside, I usually look pretty together.

Now it seems, my daughter is ready to assume her role—day-care kid with too few sprinkles on her cupcakes and a mom who can't make it to her big day. She asked if I would be there as I was getting out of the car at the train station, where my husband drops me off each morning before dropping the kids at day care and driving forty miles to his office. The shadow of bewilderment and hurt that briefly crossed her face while she kissed me good-bye would have brought an audience to tears if it were on the big screen. And, as would be written in the script to drive the point home in case the audience missed the wounded eyes, she then asked me, in the sympathetic tone of a beleaguered coworker, to see if I could try to fit it in my schedule.

I didn't cry. I didn't throw my briefcase on the tracks, get back in the car, and say "To hell with my career." Instead I was startled. I continued the routine, kissing her and her brother, beseeching them to have a good day, closing the car door, and waving good-bye with a smile. As I walked along the train platform I thought about what I had just witnessed. This look was something new. Suddenly it seems she realizes that other kids don't spend most of their days in a day-care center, or "school" as we call it to make it sound enriching. She recognizes that she really likes those days, weekends, or "family days" as we call them to make them sound special, when she can hang out in her pj's and play with her own toys with only her little brother to fight off. She's stopped calling the five girls she plays with most her "sisters" because, though at day care they try hard to make it feel like family, she understands it isn't the same.

Until now working has been easy for me because she didn't know these things. I did, of course, but her happy nature and genuine love for her teachers and playmates convinced me that I was doing a good thing for her. Her world is larger and richer than I alone ever could have made it. Now, at four, she sees that mine is too.

So I ask, is four too young to become aware that you are not the center of your mother's life, even while you are? Happy Birthday, Amelia. Welcome to the real world.

Susan Reimer

The first picture we have of Joseph shows him tucked in the crook of my arm as I lay on a gurney. You can tell by the look on his face that he is cranking. Not crying. Not squalling like a newborn. Just cranking, He is complaining.

Two years later, the first picture of Jessica shows her propped on a pillow, eyes closed and a butterfly smile on her lips. Even asleep, she is happy.

It has been like that ever since, I tell people. Twenty years of trying to make Joe happy while Jessie drifts through our days like a playful breeze.

Wise and experienced mothers will tell you that they love all of their children the same—only different. By this I don't think they mean that they love different things about each child. I think they mean that each child requires of his parents that he be loved in a different way. I think they mean that the nature of the love relationship with each child is itself profoundly different.

That is probably as it should be—how can we have cookie-cutter feelings for beings about whom we know every (different) detail? But it is exhausting. Sometimes it requires that you be two mothers. Or one, talking out of both sides of her mouth. It is worse than fixing separate meals for picky eaters.

I must confess that I have been chasing Joseph's elusive smile all his life. And when I have failed, I have felt it was my failure. I did not raise him so much as I tread lightly around him. He has catalogued my every harsh word, my every broken promise, my every contradiction, my every crummy meal, and he can wound me any time with his perfect memory.

That newborn smile of Jessie's has only ever dimmed in the shadow of her brother's achievements. She sees each one only as her shortcoming. "But you are the nice child," we tell her. It is the family joke, but Joseph, the powerful child, the determined child, the uncompromising child, never laughs.

At times it has been as simple as saying to him " 'B's are our friends. We like 'B's on our report cards" while saying to her, " 'C' means average. There is nothing average about you."

Sometimes it has been, "Joe, just tell me. Please," while it has also been "Jessie, Mommy's ears are tired."

And sometimes, it has been listening to two sets of dreams as unconnected to any vision we have ever had of our children's future as they are from each other. The military officer and the girl who wants to give facials or have a cooking show on TV.

But those are simple adaptations—ones parents make all the time. We turn our attention from one child to another so many times in a day that sometimes I think it would be better if our heads swiveled.

I am talking about a different kind of accommodation. One that requires the heart to turn on a dime. Loving one child is as thoughtlessly easy as breathing. Loving the other requires heavy lifting and can produce a cold sweat.

Even the simple act of physical affection requires me to

move on the balls of my feet. From that moment on that pillow, Jessie's puffy cheeks have invited kissing. Her skin is as soft as warm water and as temptingly pink as cotton candy. Even as a teenager she sighs a long-suffering sigh and stands still for her parents' smooches.

Joe is all muscle and bone, sinew as taut as a bow string. He throws off power and energy in a steady current. Try to hug him, and, at best, he will counter your love with a wrestling hold. At worst, he will treat your embrace like a scratchy coat in a hot room. Only when he is ill or sleeping is he vulnerable to a stroke of his hair.

Loving her is as quick and easy as a laugh. It is like dozing in the warm sun. It is like daydreaming. Loving him requires planning. Loving him is pursuit. The goal? That he recognize how much I love him.

Do I love them differently? Obviously. Do I love one more? That is like asking which weighs more, a ton of bricks or a ton of feathers. Like any mother, I would cheerfully throw myself in front of a moving train to save them. My only regret is that I could not demonstrate that devotion repeatedly.

My children appear to share nothing but a last name and a street address. They don't even look alike. Their eyes and hair not only suggest different parents, they hint at different tribes, separate continents.

Of course I love them differently; but it is because they require it of me.

Pamela Redmond Satran

The floor was littered, as it always seemed to be, with magazines and shoes and clothes and toys and, yes, even a crumb-covered plate or two. My eighteen-month-old son was toddling along, investigating every piece of debris in his path. And where was I? I was standing there, half tracking his progress, half talking on the phone—and all feeling guilty.

I was an imperfect mother in so many ways.

My house was a pit.

I let the kid play amid the detritus.

And I wasn't even watching him all that closely while he did it.

And then suddenly I thought: Maybe this is good for him.

Maybe the random objects scattered across the floor represent an educational environment for my toddler.

Maybe it was even positive that I was letting my son move around and explore at will without interfering.

And maybe sometimes, I thought in a flash of utter blinding clarity, what you *don't* do as a parent is more effective, even better for your child, than what you do.

I know, I know, that sounds like a big fat rationalization— and maybe in the moment, that's what it was. But fifteen years later, I can testify that over time it has proven to be an epiphany that changed my parenting life.

Before that moment, I was an imperfect mother and ashamed of it.

And after, I was imperfect and proud.

I have come to believe that not only are imperfect moms as good as those that try harder to do everything right—they're often *better*. That's right: I think that imperfect parenting is superior parenting.

Of course, I don't mean that the best moms are the ones who bat their kids around, berate them and call them names. That's not imperfection, that's abuse. Nor am I including those moms who let their kids go cold or hungry, their teeth unbrushed and the homework unfinished. I'd call that neglect.

But I think it's equally damaging to be the one gluing the cotton balls to the shoe box for your child's fourth-grade diorama project. As I told my three kids, I already passed fourth grade. I'll prod them to do their homework, a couple of times. I'll help with a particularly thorny problem. But actually get in there to do the work? Or even make an excuse to the teacher if they don't understand the assignment or fail to complete it?

Better, I've discovered, to step back and let them get in trouble at school or get a lower grade if they don't finish their work. Or to throw the responsibility for teaching back on the teacher if a child is having trouble understanding something. I'm not saying I'd stand by silently and let my child fail, but I don't believe I'm helping him succeed by getting too involved in day-to-day schoolwork. Letting him do it himself, on the other hand, teaches him responsibility, organization, time management, not to mention how to get those cotton balls to stick to the top of the shoe box.

I wasn't always this assertively imperfect. With my oldest child, my only daughter, I tried very hard to be as perfect a parent as I could be. By my definition, that meant being totally in tune with her every feeling and need. I attempted to be unfailingly attentive, supportive, patient, encouraging, the wonderful mother of my own fantasies.

And what happened? To my dismay, my beautiful little girl became a total monster. She demanded constant indulgence not only from me, but from the entire world. Frustration, disappointment, rules—these all were intolerable to her. She had trouble entertaining herself for any length of time and expected unflagging admiration and attention from the adults surrounding her.

My reaction to my little tyrant? If inside I was embarrassed by my daughter's behavior, if I found my temper boiling up more often and if, as I sat smiling and clapping at the four-thousandth rendition of "Tomorrow," I just longed for escape, I tried harder and harder to hide it. What a bad mother I was, to feel so angry at my own child! And so I redoubled my efforts at perfection.

And then I hit a wall. My daughter was six, I was pregnant with my second child (the bottom-feeder-to-be), we were in the grocery store, she was whining for candy or gum or chocolatey cereal, and suddenly I found myself screaming, "No!"

Everyone in the store turned to stare at me. Everyone looked shocked—especially my child. I don't think she had ever heard that word before. I certainly couldn't remember ever having said it to her, at least not with such brio. As I felt my cheeks flame up in shame, I imagined all the people thinking I was a terrible mother. And that the result of my terrible mothering was that my little girl would fall to the floor in a pond of her own tears.

But that's not what happened. What happened was that my daughter, rather than escalating her demands as she usually did, shrugged and said, "Okay."

I realized, following that incident, that I'd be a more effective parent if I said no sometimes instead of feeling as if I had to address my child's every wish and command. That sometimes denying her what she wanted was better than always giving in. That it even might be better for both of us if I showed my annoyance when I felt it.

After that day, I started saying no to my child a lot more often, began laying down much stricter rules, giving in to far fewer demands, even letting myself yell when the situation warranted it—in short, I became a much better parent. And my daughter became not only a better-behaved child, but a calmer, more confident one. Once I made it clear (to myself as well as to her) that I was in charge, she was free to be a little girl.

And I was free to blossom as an Imperfect Mom.

Through raising three children in the nearly twenty years since my hissy fit in the supermarket, here are some of the many Imperfect Things I have done:

- Let my kids eat dessert before or instead of a meal.
- Let them watch near-unlimited television and play violent video games.
- Blew off the PTA, the school bake sale, the principal's speech.
- Ditto: church.
- Never made them take music lessons or play sports.

- Forced them to go away to camp every summer, even if they didn't want to.
- Left them with a sitter to go away with my husband or travel for work.
- Didn't care if they cleaned their rooms.
- Let them wear whatever they wanted and have parties whenever they felt like it.
- Made them do their own laundry and prepare their own snacks.

Reading that list, I'd feel really lousy about myself, except that the evidence proves that all this slipshod parenting has been pretty darn effective. Now that my kids are twenty-two, sixteen, and twelve, the long-term effects of imperfection can be measured. At least with my children, opening the sweets cupboard and handing over the remote has inspired a level of self-control much stricter than any I'd impose. My younger son has a serious *Simpsons* habit, but I expect he'll give that up in time just like his brother and sister did.

Letting them make their own decisions about clothes and take care of their own rooms helped them to develop a sense of style. Making them handle their own laundry and cooking, and pushing them out of the nest to go to camp, taught them to be self-sufficient and independent—my daughter traveled to Nepal alone at seventeen. And leaving them with babysitters introduced them to several wonderful people who are in their lives still.

Not forcing activities on my children has led them to develop their own passions and talents. My daughter segued from the Girl Scouts to field hockey and on to French: she graduated from UC-Berkeley in three years and is living in Paris. My younger son loves acting, ice hockey, and fishing.

And what about that child who took the educational tour of the debris on our living room floor? He's a gourmet cook (thanks to the crumbs on the plates), a fashion connoisseur (the castoff clothes and shoes), and a voracious reader (the old magazines and newspapers). And though I can't decisively credit letting him play in the garbage for this, he just got a perfect score on the SATs.

Part V: Great Expectations

The greatest part of our happiness or misery depends on our dispositions and not on our circumstances.

— MARTHA WASHINGTON

Jacquelyn Mitchard

A few years back, when I was rather newly widowed (and yet, it had been long enough that my husband's death would no longer prevent anyone from daring even to *raise* the subject), I was expelled from the car pool.

It wasn't unexpected: I'd been on waivers since the time several months earlier when I was fifteen minutes late for pickup after school.

It had been the usual hectic, patched-together day for a mother who worked at home, trying to make it full time as a magazine writer, working part time at the university, and fussing over the idea of a novel.

I'd spent five of those lost minutes putting air in the tire of my car, a Chevy Caprice with a 350 V-8 engine that my father had sold to me. My dad then was a village official near Chicago, and the car had formerly been a police car. The white bits had been painted black, but the sound of the engine was still inappropriate to our tidy street of modest medium-density houses — a fact that caused me no little distress when I revved up at seven-thirty in the morning. Using backroads, I sped toward the school. Then, I'd had to spend another five minutes doing everything but sign an affidavit for the guard at the school gate that I was not trying to sneak in and park without a sticker.

By the time I reached the circular drive, I was sweating.

Many things have changed in the world, but a nun tapping her foot can still instantly halt your digestive processes, and that was what happened to me when I came careening into the parking lot. The good sister, standing at the curb, gave me a stern and unwavering gaze. There beside her were four other pairs of equally accusing but younger eyes, my own children's angry, the others' anxious.

I got the phone call that evening.

It was from the father of the child around the corner, the one I always picked up first. The dad was usually finishing up his morning run when I lurched into his driveway, my hair uncombed, my Bucky Badger sweatshirt tugged down over my pajama pants. His wife would be waiting at the door with his coffee and a kiss. Their serenity never failed to squeeze my heart. She was room mother for the kindergarten class, and didn't work "except at raising strong, wise, decent human beings." She often told me that she wished it were a privilege other mothers could afford. She announced this so often and with such rectitude that I wanted to ask her if she had taken a class in it, as she had taken a class in scrapbooking. *Scrapbooking*, I would grumble to myself, good grief. Could there possibly be some arcane skill involved in applying a little glue to the backs of some newspaper clippings and photos and stamping little pencils around the edges of the pages? Or was it that I really felt guilty that my own scrapbooking on my children's behalf was of the two-pocket folder variety—though I did manage to tape a letter to the outside of each year's folder, describing that kid's achievements?

Tender letters notwithstanding, I knew these folders, unlike the scrapbooks the other mothers were compiling, would not be displayed on the table at the graduation festivities, the last page being the acceptance letter from Stanford.

I wondered if there would ever be an acceptance letter from Stanford, or even from a minor branch of the state university.

I wondered whether there would be any newspaper clippings at all for my children, frankly—the kind that would read, "Edgebrook's Quarterback Assures State Bid" or even "Edgebrook Student Wins State Spelling Bee." So recently bereaved, and—our income sliced in half—bedraggled had my children become that sometimes, it was all they could do to go to school, much less compete for honors.

On the night that I committed the car-pool coup de grace, the jogging father explained, "This just isn't working out. It's too bad. I know you have a lot of challenges, but it's important to my kids and to us that they get to and from school on time."

"I know," I replied with a sigh, "It's important to me, too. It just . . . doesn't always happen that way."

"Well, we have to make it happen that way for us, and so we've had to put together another arrangement," he told me, not unkindly.

"Oh," I said. "I see."

I hung up and decided I didn't care.

But I did.

The call and its message—yet another way in which I'd managed to fall short—sent a sliver into the little space under my heart, into the place where I'd once tried to store solid, burnished proof that, despite our woes and my work, our family was just the same as every other family in our neighborhood. Just as nuclear. Just as integrated.

Just as healthy.

There were a lot of slivers in that place, and I'd managed to buff most of them out with grit.

Well, sort of.

It had been a year since the time I'd cried all afternoon after a school counselor phoned to inform me that I was an ambitious career woman who wasn't bothering to count the costs to her family. My kids had been troubled, obviously, when I'd had to enlist a slew of different family members to stay with them while I went away for two weeks to finish my book (preceded in our family by the adjectives "dumb old"). During that time I was away, my four-year-old called me nightly, fearful that, I, too, would die and never come home. A neighbor had observed another of my children using a hose to drench his brother from a second-story bedroom window. My eldest boy was caught stealing a pencil from the school store and, under sympathetic questioning, blurted, "Well, at least my mom'll pay attention to this!" He'd also used olive oil to make a skating rink for our ferrets on the kitchen linoleum.

"You need to find another line of work, if you want to raise normal children," the school psychologist told me. I'd bitten my tongue. What I wanted was to tell *him* he needed to find another line of work.

I mean, would he have said this to a single father? If that father had taken a risk in hopes of not only providing his children with a better future but trying to prove it was important to soldier on after a loss? Would he have said this to Andy Griffith—told him to give up being the sheriff of Mayberry and become a telemarketer so Opie wouldn't feel neglected? And, right, I *didn't* have an Aunt Bea, or an aunt at all, or a mother or a mother-in-law. I had a teenaged helper and a college-aged intern who was addicted to personal phone calls (to San Diego). And yes, both of whom usually had their cars warming up in preparation for their departure when I stumbled in at five in the evening on the nights I worked at the university.

I wanted to tell him it wasn't easy.

But I couldn't. Or more properly, I wouldn't.

Still, I got over that, just as I got over it when a coworker at a baby shower told me, "At this point, I'm just glad to have a happy husband and healthy children. Other women might have concerns they *think* are more important. But that's mine." I felt as if she believed that I'd *decided* to have my husband die young and *chosen* to have my children be nervous and inattentive in school, and that writing a book was just about the most frivolous thing a good mother could do. Instead of sticking up for myself and everyone else who had to do it on her own, I felt guilty.

And now, here I was, a certifiable outcast, a car-pool reject.

"It's not your fault," said my son, Rob, then in sixth grade, after I informed him that our school car pool now consisted of him, me, and our car. "I could help you more so you wouldn't forget your lists and your keys and stuff."

"It is my fault," I told him. "I'm the mother. You already help too much. You're a kid, not a grown-up."

I wasn't nailing up a cross for myself. But my failure to line up the ducks, despite four telephone answering machines and five calendars, was not new. It was, however, as vexing and incomprehensible to me as it was to other people. I would think all was trundling along just swell, and then . . . oops! There I'd be, listening to the exasperation in the voice at the other end of the phone from the dentist's office, the piano teacher, the Scout troop meeting . . . golly, right, sure! We couldn't have forgotten . . . oh, dear. Yes, I had. I was sorry. I was so sorry. I should have planned ahead. I should have done something different. But there was no manual for achieving excellence in widowed motherhood, only for grieving it.

Take the night before the day I was expelled.

I knew the nature of the day just ahead. I knew that two of my four children would be home because there was no preschool that day. I knew I would be having a visitor from out of town. That would mean many opportunities for error, for possible stitches dropped in the routine. Other mothers would have done more organizing on that night before, instead of selfishly letting everyone, even the one-year-old sit up and watch *X-Files* just so as to have someone to talk it over with. Other mothers might have begged a friend to stand in for car pool, admitting they could not perform, just that one day, as ably solo instead of tandem. Other mothers wouldn't even have *had* the one-year-old. I had insisted on adopting her as a single parent just a year after my husband, Dan, died, in defiance of the best advice of loving friends and family—when I didn't even have enough money to fix the hole in the roof.

But not following my heart's desire, bravely, despite the seeming foolishness of the choice, would have meant admitting that all the king's horses and all the king's men couldn't make us whole again.

I wouldn't do that. One person can only do so much.

But had I been more cautious, lived smaller, been less impulsive, that last car-pool morning would not have come up like thunder. I would not have overslept, never having quite mastered the radio alarm clock after my husband's death. There would not have been a crazy scramble—lost lunches, lost gloves, lost tempers. I would not have had to ask myself, should I change the baby now, or just throw on her snowsuit? I wouldn't have had to chase a lost ferret or stop, the clock hands already signaling an ominous message, to sign for the package from UPS. I would have noticed that mushy tire.

But I didn't, and I was late.

Why *couldn't* I do it? It was only one week each month.

Why couldn't I prove that I was okay, the same Jackie, and that nothing was going to change for my kids, despite the loss of their dad and their mother's decision to try to wrestle down grief by doing something as nuts and doomed to failure as writing a book.

But the night I was kicked out of the car pool was a turning point. I realized I had to face grim facts.

I didn't really blame the other parents, and they didn't really blame me. But they looked down on me, just a little. Now, I was no poster child for the afflictions of single motherhood. I had the privilege of being able to work at home, in my own business, at least half the time. I had the privilege of being able to pay a little for a little help in the home. I worked hard for that.

But it was still so easy to stretch it nearly transparent from having so much ground to cover.

And once upon a time, not very long ago, I thought that night, I wouldn't have been able to completely understand why things didn't work so well for me as for my neighbors—both families made up of two parents and two children. I knew that two-on-two works better than one on four—which amounts to zone defense. But I could not have helped feeling I'd had my life a little better sorted out, back when I was able to buy matching Christmas sweaters for my boys and alphabetize my books.

Once upon a time, though I didn't really *pity* single moms, I didn't really think they had to be so darned sloppy. It was a little vexing. When divorced moms Leah or Ellen or Lynn showed up late for the game, trailing soccer clothes fresh from the dirty-laundry hamper, I would think, these sisters need to set better priorities. I would wonder why they didn't cut out the fat, those volleyball clubs or book groups or Margarita Thursdays. I couldn't believe it when they tried to have dates!

I didn't realize how lonely a person could be.

But a year or so after Dan died, dating was no longer the last thing on my mind.

However, it quickly slipped to the back of the minds of men I met when they learned how many children I had. I told myself I didn't care about that, either. So there.

Everywhere I went, I went with my posse of short people, and when I saw tired moms hand off the sleeping toddler onto a sturdier shoulder, I would try to stand taller and heft my own sleeping toddler higher, as though her weight wouldn't make my arms ache next morning.

When I hollered so loud at my youngest son that my pal across the street complained, I could have told him the truth — that I'd lost my temper and banged so hard on the filing cabinet with a shoe that I knocked the jar containing my husband's ashes off onto the floor and had to spend an hour first cleaning out the Dustbuster, then vacuuming the ashes up. But then, my neighbor would have thought I was nuts, unable to cope. I could have told him that sometimes, at that time, things got so out of hand I didn't notice that my middle child had spray-painted our rock garden gold so that everyone on the street would believe we were rich, because it was so obvious to others that we weren't that they anonymously left boxes of their kids' old clothes on my doorstep. But fessing up would have meant that my family was like my car—no longer what it used to be, but painted so that no one could tell.

It took me two full years at full tilt, falling farther and farther behind the standards of my friends, who had perennial gardens and *knitted* their matching Christmas sweaters in October so the photo for the cards would be ready for the holidays, to realize that there was no shame in being what I was. I was a sometimes not-so-hot mother and a not-at-all successful two-in-one parent. And I worked. It took me even longer to recognize how unfair I had been to single parents when I wasn't one. It took me longer still to realize that nothing, no matter what advantages she might have, is ever quite on kilter for a single parent who works. That's because what a working single mother has to do is work and be single and a mother, and one person can only do so much.

I remembered reading old magazine stories about Mia Farrow's legendary tribe of fourteen, with seven still at home. People called her both fuzzy-headed and out of touch with reality.

Anyone, people said, could do it with live-in nannies and lots of bucks.

But even after I'd written a book and made some bucks—not movie-star bucks, but enough to build myself a room over the garage and trade in my old police car for a minivan—things didn't really, profoundly change. I was still one parent shy of a full load. When the buck stops—when there's trouble at school, or a kid gets sick enough that a less harried and therefore more noticing parent would have noticed—the buck stops with the parent. At the end of the day, whatever else she does in her life, the parent is the one really responsible. And single parents, even ones who try, as I did, to hold up the sky—even with both hands—simply can't. Money or paid helpers can only prop up, but can never really repair a structure that has significant design flaws. A table is meant to have four legs. Frank Lloyd Wright's tables had three and they were very graceful, but they fell over. Relatives are darling. Friends are loyal. But only one person loves a child the way a parent does. And families of four stand up under pressure better with two parents. Otherwise, things fall over.

In fact, I didn't stop being chronically late or having to request triple copies of field trip permissions slips or waking up terrified for no reason I could pinpoint or refusing permission to take an exercise class until after I married—five years after Dan died. I married a terrific guy I never dated because I didn't have time to date. We met only because he helped build that office over my garage, and, though younger than I am by a dozen years, he was getting frightened that he wouldn't marry in time to have the big family he'd hoped for. He married one.

Now, I have six kids, and a busy life, busier than most, but also more manageable. I don't need the kind of string for my memory that preschoolers need for their mittens. If I didn't have a school bus stop near my driveway—and a son with a driver's license to step in for emergencies—I could show up on time for the car pool, because someone would have my back on the days when things tipped over.

But I won't ever forget being expelled from the car pool.

Though I now tell it as a funny story, I won't forget the shame I felt, and that my kids probably felt, and the shame the other parents must have known that I felt. I still remember the pain I feel now because I never, ever wondered why divorced moms (there were no other widows my age) didn't shape up and show up. And you know what? I still wonder why the other parents in the car pool didn't just give me a pass, as a sort of gesture of good karma. I wonder, too, how many single parents I've helped out and how many I haven't. I wonder how many times I've overlooked doing just one small thing—such as taking over her car-pool week and brushing it off as nothing so she didn't feel embarrassed—and might have helped someone else who was trying, and probably failing, to do way, way too much?

My kids grew older.

And none of them has gone to Stanford. But one came within a single "W" of winning the state spelling bee; and one's won a national acting competition; and one, who has major learning disabilities, got a B on the physics final; and one reads two years above her grade level. These are not big deals to the world, but they prove to me I didn't do all of it wrong. One of the other moms I knew long ago is raising a little granddaughter, though her eldest is only a sophomore in high school; and one has a kid in rehab. One has a kid at Harvard but lives with a professor twenty years older than she is; and one has a kid who was headed for Texas A&M on a football scholarship when he committed a crime that sent him, instead, to boot camp. This proves nothing about the quality of their parenthood except that I learned earlier than they did how it feels to wake up terrified. I hear about them, and about how they try to paper over their fears, as I tried. And I wish they'd just be braver than I was and let it out. I wish they'd ask for help. But I know why they don't.

Looking back, I guess I could have said to the other carpoolers, who were, after all, decent people, please, just help me out for a few months. Let my kid ride along when you go. I'll make it up to you somehow, someday.

I could have said, I know it looks as though I'm too wacky and busy and unorganized to take care of my own—but I'm not doing any of this on purpose.

I didn't, though.

There are only so many things one person can do.

Teme Weinstein Ring

When I was healthy and striving to be Single Super Mom, I took pride in all I did: went to law school, coached Little League, wore cute clothes, traveled with my sons and allowed them to hold raucous sleepovers (which went well, save for the time I discovered children sleeping in the fireplace). When my boys were eleven and nine years old, I became ill with myalgic encephalopathy (also known as chronic fatigue syndrome). I felt I'd gone from Super Mom to Pooper Mom.

I went from list maker to listless. My formerly indefatigable self was awash in exhaustion. I developed severe dysautonomia—a partial breakdown of the neurological system. When I stood, my blood pressure plummeted and my heart fluttered and pounded like butterflies dribbling basketballs. Breathing was suddenly arduous. I sounded the way I imagine Darth Vader would, were he to suck up Pop Rocks with a Crazy Straw.

I was too weak to negotiate the twenty-five feet between my bed and the bathroom. Grocery shopping, with its solar system–like distance between the parking lot and essentials such as milk, became impossible. I felt as if Wile E. Coyote had used an Acme plastic surgery kit to perform liposuction on my energy.

Worse than the physical discomfort, I felt I'd failed as a

mother. Front-yard games of catch became memories. Gone were spontaneous trips to watch the Cubs warm up at Wrigley Field. No more invitations to "as many friends as you want" for weekend-long sleepovers (which usually went well, save for the time one guest ordered hundreds of dollars' worth of pizza and magnanimously charged it to his dad's credit card).

Dinner planning, never one of my strong points, went from less-than-Emeril to ephemeral. Short-lived and barely there. My pre-illness dinner repertoire consisted of fish sticks, scrambled eggs, and on extra ambitious evenings, pancakes. But in this new world, dinnertime found me too woozy to lift my head, let alone to bustle (even ineptly) around the kitchen.

Fortunately, it was a safe walk for my kids to pick up dinner from the Great Chicken Disaster (not its real name, but that's what I called our local takeout on one brain-foggy evening and the misnomer stuck). We did dine with captains and counts, however. Okay, I admit it. It was Cap'n Crunch and Count Chocula.

During those first years of illness, I felt terribly guilty, wracked with imperfection. Many nights I sat bolt upright in bed, fretting about my absence from PTA meetings, my inability to chauffeur the boys to lessons, and my failure to appear perfectly put together (or at least, to avoid sporting lank hair and pajamas at three in the afternoon).

Because my exhaustion, faintness, and headaches were so unpredictable, I dreaded anything that required scheduling. Parent-teacher conferences, dentist appointments, and car pools required a reliability that I could no longer offer. My spirit was willing—always—but my body was as uncooperative as an angry toddler in a car seat.

I confess that at times I resorted to subterfuge. Take car pool (please!). Our school offered no bus service and was not within walking distance. Getting into a car pool was similar to gaining early admission to Yale. You competed with gaggles of other anxious families, and success depended on starting months in advance and on presenting a cheery can-do spirit.

I knew that on most days I was unable to drive. But feeling desperate, I negotiated car-pool admittance without disclosing my limitations. I gambled, hoping that my car-pool responsibilities would coincide with my better days. At least, being in a car pool would guarantee reliable rides for my kids during most of the week.

The times the gamble didn't pay off are etched in my memory. I remember frantic SOS calls to friends, other busy moms whose heavy loads did not always allow them to take on mine. Several times, my sons' stepmother responded with extraordinary grace to my awkward requests and drove for me. Once I called a taxi and in an exhausted fog, rode shotgun, unsure if I could trust the driver alone with the precious cargo. When the bright yellow cab pulled into the school's car-pool line behind the station wagons and minivans, the children were agog. I was mortified. (How appallingly imperfect I was, for my children and all the world to see.)

Facing our maternal imperfections touches some sort of raw primal nerve. The world is busting-out full with hazards and opportunities. Good moms, we tell ourselves, empower their children to escape the former and to embrace the latter. If we perform this mission imperfectly, will we shove our kids into harm's way? Deprive them of well-adjusted adulthood? Our gut answer seems to be yes and yes. Maybe nature hardwired us this way to ensure human survival. If we reach for the stars, our children are less likely to fall in life's mud.

I think we also feel pressure to present a perfect face to our children. If they witness our vulnerability, the times we're swept onto life's rocky shoals, perhaps they'll think less of us. They'll think less of life.

These were my fears when I became ill.

Do you ever say, "I wish I could go back, knowing what I know now"? That's how I feel. I wish I could travel back through time to those first baffling years of disability and reassure myself that, incredibly, our life would turn out far better than I expected. I wish I had known that by witnessing my health struggles, my sons would become young men of uncommon good character.

When I was well, I thought I had to be a perfect mom. Back then, being perfect meant doing a lot, doing everything. Keeping the house clean. Holding down a high-powered job. Presiding over sleepovers (which sometimes went well, save for the "movie night incident" when the VCR broke early on and before I could say, "Rumble in The Bronx," twelve boys were hopping about in sleeping bags, vaulting my furniture).

I now realize that it's not doing a lot, but being a lot that counts. Nine years later, I have two sons who are everything I'd hoped. As they were growing up, I was unable to attend to housework. They learned to do their own laundry and not to fear dust bunnies who grew faster than they did. I was unable to prepare meals. They learned, well okay, to dial for takeout, but soon afterward, to cook for themselves and for me. They learned to be resourceful. I had to halt my career plans; my sons learned flexibility. I was often unable to drive; the boys learned independence. I needed more assistance than most moms; my sons became compassionate.

I learned that tackling chronic illness takes time; that in life I was going to be more tortoise than hare. My sons learned patience. And the importance of doing their best.

Some things I didn't teach well. I hate asking for help. They do, too. I sometimes tell them I feel fine when I don't. I know they sometimes tell me they feel fine when they don't. We still have work to do.

I found out that I was imperfect. I learned to forgive myself. And to forge on. I may not be Super Mom, but no longer do I feel like Pooper Mom. I've settled on Trooper Mom. I've learned to be imperfect with grace. It is perhaps the best lesson a mom can give.

Katherine Lee

~~~~~~

Even before my son was born, I tried to make things as perfect for him as possible in this imperfect world. I ate at least three balanced meals a day, cut out all sweets and caffeine, and did prenatal yoga regularly in an effort to provide him with a relaxed environment in which to grow. When I was at last able to hold my baby in my arms, I whispered to him, tears welling, my throat swollen thick with happiness, these primal promises: to always love him, to be there for him in whatever way he needed me, and to try to be the best mother I could be.

Now, three years later, I am an overworked, often-stressed, sleep-deprived mother who breathes a sigh of relief whenever my imaginative little boy immerses himself in his toy cars for a few minutes so that I can answer some e-mails or return a few phone calls. As a freelance writer and editor working from home, I feel the pull of work when we're finger-painting but feel like a soldier gone AWOL when he's with a babysitter and I'm at my desk. There are nights when takeout is what's for dinner and I'm just too tired to handle his tantrums like the patient, beatific, Julie Andrews–mother I want to be and instead end up resembling a shrieking harridan more along the lines of

Cruella De Vil. More often than not, I feel like my best isn't my best, and it just isn't good enough.

As a former editor at *Parenting* magazine, I know all too well how moms can often be the lightning rod for parenting issues in our society. Every day, somewhere, in some form, the debate rages on over whether or not moms should work or stay at home, whether we should always choose breast over the bottle, whether we should let our babies cry it out or sleep in our beds. But speaking from personal experience, the harshest critics seem to be, in the end, ourselves. If there's anything that can match the heights of mother-love, it's the depths of mother-guilt.

Like most mothers I know, I blame myself when my son catches a cold or falls down on the playground. I should've stopped the playdate when I saw that his friend had the sniffles, even though they were having fun. I should've told him to slow down and not run so fast in his new shoes. I should've *known*. I should've *seen*.

Two years ago, when my husband told me on the telephone on his way to work that he was leaving me, I felt many things: shock, disbelief, numbness. Pain so searing that my heart literally did ache, and I discovered for the first time the full measure of what that word can really mean. As the weeks and months wore on and it became clear that my husband was indeed gone, I gazed around at the remains of my life and our shattered future, and there was, inevitably, guilt. How could I have so completely trusted and loved someone for thirteen years, enough to close my eyes and sleep next to him every night, enough to say to him, "Yes, let's do it. Let's start a family," and have been so surprised? How could I not have *seen*?

When I think about my situation logically, I know that we can't always know what's secreted away in someone else's heart, and we can't fix their demons or make choices for them no matter how much we love them. But when I look around the playground on the weekends or take Sam to birthday parties and we are surrounded by intact families—a mother, a father, siblings—I feel responsible for choosing the wrong mate and for not being able to give my son a mother and a father behind his stroller, at the dinner table, on lazy Sunday mornings. Yes, children can and do thrive in homes where there is only one parent, and yes, they are resilient and can grow up to be happy when their mothers and fathers decide to separate. But the fact is that I had envisioned a different world for my son— not of overnights with dad and shuttling back and forth between two homes—but a life in which he and his sister or brother would go to sleep every night in their beds, secure in the love that binds their family together. No matter how many times I try to tell myself it's not my fault, no matter how many times my family and friends say they couldn't see it either, that no one could really have known, I look at my beautiful little boy and want to tell him how sorry I am. I couldn't make his world perfect, after all. I couldn't stop our little family from breaking apart.

It's a frightening thought—that I can't stop bad things from happening to me much less to the people I love. But that's the reality of life: to love is scary, for in loving, you risk losing. I am learning to surrender to that fact, and trying to remember that what really counts are the promises I made to my son just hours after he was born. Even if nothing else I do is perfect, my love for my child is. Of that, I am certain.

Deborah Caldwell

~~~~~~

I am what you might charitably call a lenient mother. My two sons—ages nine and six—watch a lot of ESPN and Nickelodeon on TV, stay up past ten half the week, eat in the living room, walk around outside in their socks, make a dog's breakfast of my Honda's backseat, and leave clothes on their bedroom floors.

Every once in a while, I let them have a "backward dinner," which consists of ice cream as the first course and the rest of dinner afterward. You have guessed correctly if you just said to yourself, "No way do they always get to the rest of dinner."

I once let the boys use a hand saw (okay, but it was a really small one) to build a "garage" for their numerous tiny vehicles. After they'd strolled down the building materials aisle at Home Depot with me, they got so excited by the concept of carpentry that I let them buy wood slats to try out at home. Unfortunately, after a day of measuring, sawing, and nailing, the garage project was abandoned on the back porch, its leftovers in a heap by the door. I did put the saw away, however—but only after one of my friends pointed out that it was, um, not a great thing to have a sharp object languishing near potential bare feet.

Of course, my friend has two daughters, so I can understand how alarming my boy-centered household seems. I grew up in a girl house—Barbies, pink bedrooms, menstrual cycles, glitter, ballerina dresses—but I now live with pee on the toilet seat, stinky feet on the couch, and baseball gloves on the kitchen floor. Every time I play catch with my sons, I tempt fate. One time my older son pitched a whiffle ball at me and hit me in the nose. I reeled backward on the lawn in pain. With the three of us playing recently, the little one chucked a baseball my way and hit me directly in the heart. He later tried to convince me his brother threw the offending ball. (At least my older son kept asking me if I could breathe.)

A couple weeks ago, I pulled onto our street in the car, only to witness my six-year-old riding his bike like a circus per-former—hands on the handlebars, both feet on the seat, and no helmet. Thank God we live on a cul-de-sac. The neighbors couldn't have missed it—along with the ball throwing, lawn wrestling, and downhill driveway skateboarding that occurs regularly around here.

The low point came on a late-spring morning a few months ago. I was wearing a twenty-year-old terry robe, I hadn't yet showered, and my hair was a rat's nest. The doorbell rang and I answered it. There stood my eighty-five-year-old next-door neighbor. He had an issue to discuss about a two-foot-square patch of grass that borders our yards—it had been partially de-nuded by boy foot traffic. I swear, the patch was minuscule. And although he technically owned the patch, it was so far into my yard that I might as well have owned it. Nevertheless, I apologized profusely and promised to buy sod.

Then he delivered the blow: "You're too permissive as a par-ent," he said, narrowing his eyes and—this really happened—

jabbing his index finger at me. Once again I apologized, more horrified than angry. After I closed the door behind him, I swallowed back tears. He was right, and I hated it. They may be boys, but I really am a permissive parent. Another of my friends—who has four children with whom she travels the world with her diplomat husband and nanny—once described her own parenting style as "so laissez-faire as to be neglectful." At the time, my older boy was a baby and I was still in the stage of motherhood that involves grinding homemade baby food and feeling smug.

At the time I thought I would never be laissez-faire. Of course, I couldn't comprehend how complicated her life was. But eventually my boys got older, and my own life got complicated. About a year ago, my husband and I separated after sixteen years of marriage. At heart, I am still a small-town minister's daughter who believes in marriage, motherhood, and apple pie. I feel guilty for the divorce, guilty for letting my kids eat Jolly Ranchers on a daily basis, guilty that I can't be a minivan-driving soccer mom. In fact, I wake every day shocked that I'm a single mother. I was once so very traditional—sure of how to control my life and my boys' little lives as well. Now I have joined the flawed and sinful human race.

Because I am a small-town minister's daughter, however, I have become obsessed with finding redemption. That's not easy when other parents monitor their kids' sugar intake, hire after-school tutors, and join the PTA. In my dreams. Most of the time I'm just slogging along and hoping for the best.

And yet . . . both boys excel in school. They behave flawlessly in church, and the older one even sings hymns. They eat broccoli without complaint. They always say thank you. They help me clean (but only general household messes—not their own). They will on occasion help me cook. I can trust the nine-year-old enough to let him stay home while I drive into town for a quick errand. They play tenderly with neighborhood toddlers. They help me hang pictures. They rub my neck and ask how I'm doing when they sense I'm exhausted. They ask for hugs and talks on their beds. They are universally described as good boys who listen well. They even sometimes tell me they love me. Occasionally I surmise that I would have been permissive even if I weren't a single mother. I'm just a lily-livered pushover who can't follow advice books and toughen up. And then I look at the two miracles growing before my eyes and think laissez-faire might not be a bad way to be after all.

Nancy Bilyeau

~~~~~~

It seemed like just another nugget of bad news in the paper. "Rocket fuel has been found in surprisingly high levels in mothers' breast milk," I read, sitting at my messy desk, sipping my second towering coffee of the morning. Then a certain sentence jumped off the page: "These levels of rocket fuel could even cause developmental delays in children."

I set the paper down next to my Mac computer, the Starbucks turned sour in the back of my throat. *Is that it?* I asked myself. *Did I eat food laced with rocket fuel when I was pregnant? Is that the reason why?*

At his private elementary school, just six blocks from my midtown Manhattan magazine office, my son Alex was at that moment heading into morning reading group. Six and a half years old, he can read about twenty words and sound others out with his patented determination. His math skills are strong too: he can add and is beginning to subtract. He loves science and computers and art. He lives for Saturday soccer.

And yet all is not as it should be. My son has "issues." Developmental issues. He had but five words at the age of two; he doesn't speak with proficiency now. He has trouble relating to children his own age without professional prompting. At the playgrounds on the weekends, other little boys will scramble up to Alex, often busy digging an ambitious tunnel in the sandbox, and eagerly ask, "Do you want to play?" Alex smiles, but he doesn't make a reply or stop what he's doing. About a minute later, Alex will peer around, then ask me: "Where's the boy?" My heart breaking a bit, I'll say, "He's gone, Alex." In the Darwinian stew of the playground, children have three seconds to respond to one another's social cues. Alex misses by a mile.

When people ask me where my son goes to school and I tell them Alex attends a small special-ed school, the next question is: "What's wrong?" And then comes the confusing part: I don't even know. In the offices of various "experts"—the pediatric neurologists and psychologists, the speech therapists, occupational therapists and play therapists—I have sat and discussed the problems of my son. And nearly every time come away with a different diagnosis: He has PDD-OS, he has ADD, he has Asperger's. He is an "out-of-sync" child, with sensory issues. He has low tone. He has a budding anxiety disorder. Some of these things cancel one another out. One neurologist who commanded the sum of $2,500 for an evaluation admitted that PDD-OS, Alex's most common diagnosis, which stands for "pervasive development delays, not otherwise specified," is a "garbage diagnosis." "It means no one is certain what's wrong with the child," she said.

Alex's pediatrician, Dr. Michael Traister, a warm and pragmatic Upper West Side doctor, veers away from labels and stresses the positives: Alex is making steady progress. He talks more. He makes eyes contact. Dr. Traister is one of the only cheerleaders in our lives.

"I've never seen a child like Alexander before," hissed the

director of his private preschool when he was four years old. My son's debut in the world of education was an unmitigated disaster. After one week, my husband and I were sitting in the director's office with a consultant child psychologist whose first question was: "Is Alexander premature?" (He was actually born four days past his due date.) It went downhill from there. Seven weeks after he began preschool, on the eve of Halloween and Alex's excitedly donning a firefighter's costume, the director informed me over the phone that a group of other parents had descended on her office and demanded that Alex be removed. He was taking up too much of the teacher's time, time that was being stolen from *their* children. I disintegrated into deep, painful sobs and met my husband at home. Enraged, he stormed over to the preschool and ripped Alex's name off the cubicle and gathered all of his little belongings. We withdrew Alex from the school. *You can't fire us! We quit!*

We hurled all of our savings at therapists in a desperate campaign to move Alex forward. None of the good ones in Manhattan, the therapists with a track record, would take my insurance. This was a cash-only enterprise. My then-employer, Ellen Levine, editor in chief of *Good Housekeeping*, sympathetically allowed me one day off a week for one month to shuttle my son around to the experts' offices. At the same time, my husband and I devoured *Late Talking Children*, by economist Thomas Sowell, himself the parent of a child with serious language delays. Sowell makes a persuasive case that many such children are actually gifted in math, science, and music (Einstein being the poster child). Labeling them as developmentally delayed and treating them as such hurts this type of child rather than helps. "Alex is *smart*," my husband and I told each other over and over. "He is a late bloomer." We saw a cheerful, humorous boy, gorgeous with dark blond hair and blue eyes, who relished "Spot" books, James Taylor tunes, and a perfectly prepared grilled-cheese sandwich. The world saw a loser.

Although I worked full time, I stayed involved in his therapies. The office of Alex's speech therapist, who charged $1,200 a month for twice-a-week sessions, was a block from *Good Housekeeping,* and on my lunch hours I sometimes attended the end of a session. The therapist would sigh over Alex's condition: "You've got to get him into a program this fall." The way she said the word *program* signaled special ed, and I wasn't ready for that. Although Alex would be turning five over the summer, I wanted to get him into another preschool, give him one more year to catch up. When I was growing up in the Midwest, special-ed kids were subjected to unending torment. I didn't want that for Alex. Sometimes, as I walked back to my office from the therapist's office, it was hard to put one foot in front of another. I felt as if the world were pressing down on me.

Alongside my fear and worry and depression I was still tormented by the word *why.* Were my genes lousy? Had I not eaten well enough while pregnant? Was it those three glasses of wine I drank before I even knew I was pregnant? If I had coached and prompted Alex more as a toddler would he be so far behind? My husband had stayed home with our son his first three years, taking him to the park and playground every day, no matter the weather, to let our high-energy boy run it off. Would he have done better with nannies? Had we hopelessly bungled it?

"It's neurological," Alex's play therapist told me quietly one day when I wept over my unanswered questions. "It's nothing you've done or haven't done." But it was hard to let myself off the hook.

One day I asked a new friend about her preteen daughter who attended a special-ed high school in Manhattan. I had to know whether she had hesitated to do it. The answer was yes — when the girl was younger, Alex's age, my friend and her husband had been confident she would grow out of it. She was a late bloomer, they thought. It took years of denial, and the girl's struggling in school, before a special school was considered. Once she got the right help, she thrived. Alex was oblivious to his perceived issues and delays. But that wouldn't last forever.

After some teary talks, my husband and I followed up on a pamphlet for a new school for kids with learning delays. The director of Aaron School greeted us heartily at the front door for our parents' tour; Alex was accepted a month or so later. Our son is now in the middle of his second year, and we've been given no reason to believe he won't mainstream someday.

I still wake up in the middle of the night and ask why. I can't seem to make peace with the fact that there are no clear answers to this. Maybe it's the journalist in me. I crave the tidy explanation. But while I wrestle with it, we all move forward. And hope.

Part VI: Past Imperfect

You will wear many hats—
including that of lifelong learner.

— GRETA NAGEL

Gabrielle Erickson

~~~~~~

Imperfect, *moi*? Uh, let me count the ways I blew it with my three sons: Buying too many dippy toys and allowing too much dopey TV. Yelling too much. Not learning early about setting limits and offering consequences. Being nosy and overprotective. Not understanding—let alone encouraging—healthy risk-taking. Not helping them develop much of a relationship with my crazy but lovable side of the family. Not teaching them service to community. Keeping a cluttered and messy house.

That's just for starters. But right now, what worries me is that I haven't taught my three sons, Eli, twenty-three, Adam, nineteen, and Daniel, fifteen, enough practical know-how. My large extended family is populated with men and boys who know how to do all kinds of stuff—groom horses, change a car's oil, repair furniture, split firewood. At twelve, I could drive a farm tractor, knew how to mix the pigs' feed, and, one November, was in charge of cooking and planning meals for my father and foster sister for two weeks when my mother went to stay with my sister after the birth of her first child. I sort of wanted that kind of expertise for my kids.

Not happening. Not on my watch, anyway. Daniel, I'm embarrassed to say, was the last kid in his first-grade class to learn to tie his shoes. Why? Because I have limited patience for basics. In my view, kids should be born knowing how to boil water, tie their shoes, and fry an egg. This, I know, is not fair. Confession: I have often had trouble not regarding them (this is awful, I know, but it is truth time here) as stupid little adults—who ought to just know stuff. This, I realized belatedly and regretfully, is terribly unkind, not to mention misguided and ignorant, but there you are. We all come into parenthood with baggage, and this was a big piece of mine—it was how my parents, bless their dear, departed, forgiven hearts—treated me. Parenthood, much desired and even fought for, came hard for me. I had to invent it all. The emotional energy that took didn't leave a lot for lessons in, say, the difference between a Phillips screwdriver and a flathead, or how to repair a broken dining room chair.

I have to say that some of the problem has to be my own ego. I do lots of things well, and like to. It was easier to just do things than to teach them how. I confused getting the job done with enjoying—and letting them enjoy and learn and be frustrated by—the *process* of fixing and creating and doing. I wish I'd slowed down and let them help me cook dinner sometimes, when they were small and interested in that sort of thing. We could have had fun, and they would have learned how to get a meal on the table. Ditto gathering information for prospective family vacations. Wouldn't they have been more interested in the summer trip if I'd sat them down in the dead of winter with a pile of brochures and maps? I missed the chapter of the how-to-parent manual that said part of self-esteem is self-reliance.

God knows I didn't want my boys to get competent the way I did: living in a house where the roles were backward and it was the children's job to take care of the parents. The tricky part about admitting parental imperfections is that my failures could begin to sound like theirs. Long ago I realized, as a recovering perfectionist, that the only way I could be a perfect mom would be to have perfect children. And even in the fog of early parenthood, I knew that was a bad, bad trip to lay on my beloved babes.

Besides, there are lots of things they *can* do: Eli, especially, has embraced competence since his four years off at college. He knows how to set an attractive table, iron his own clothes (I taught him about three months ago), pay his own bills. He even organized a workable lawnmowing rotation system with his brothers. Adam is a whiz at computers (full disclosure: I once called him out of his middle school lunch period to ask how to open a difficult file). He also spent some time at a private school where he learned, among other things, to sew on a button. When pressed, he can mop the kitchen as well as I can. I did manage a while ago to teach Daniel how to use the oven, and he regularly makes himself frozen pizza now. When the mom-bus is unavailable, he can find his own way around our sprawling suburban town using mass transit. Plus, he is the soul of cooperation: he'll do just about anything I ask him to. All three have been doing their own laundry since Daniel was ten, and have had regular household chores for years (working from a list I give them each week).

Still, I think that in the short time they'll all still be under my roof, I might add a few lessons: how to check the oil in the car, hammer a nail, write a check, make a doctor's appointment, buy your own underwear, fry an egg. Then again, I might not. They're older now, and have ideas of their own about what constitutes important life skills.

A friend once asked me—when I fretted that none of my

men regularly volunteered to do what needed to be done in the house—"Who put you in charge?" I'm pretty sure that the best way for my sons to learn now is for me to back off a bit. So I've made a really important decision: I'm resigning my role as CEO of toilet paper supplies. Let the chips fall where they may. In the meantime, I'll enjoy them just as they are, as imperfect in their own ways as I am (alas!) in mine.

FROM MY LITTLE PONY TO PRE-SLUT:

THE REGRETTABLE YEARS

Katharine Weber

~~~~~~

You think you're an independent, out-of-the-box thinker. Original. Someone so original that you would never use the phrase "out-of-the-box." You're thoughtful. You make good choices. You know who you are.

Then you have children. Every other choice you make for your child seems to represent a path, a belief system, an opportunity to succeed or fail, a moment of definition, each decision large or small a potential turning point in your child's life, in your family's sense of itself. Who are we? What's right for us? What comes naturally, what requires painstaking debate? Sometimes you know you're at a turning point. Sometimes you only see it in hindsight.

My daughters are both in their twenties now. They are splendid and successful women. My husband and I can feel pretty good about how they turned out. We got it right, mostly. But if I had it to do over again, I would protect my children from our insidious culture a little better, a little longer. I wouldn't so readily indulge their endless fascination with trashy teenage magazines, with glossy women's magazines. I would care more about what they watched on television, about what movies they saw when they went to other people's houses. I would think harder about which people's houses they went to. I would guard more vigilantly against the terrible pressures on girls to have certain kinds of bodies, and the even worse pressure to think about their bodies in certain ways. I would be more aware of all the things that constitute an invasion of complexities and confusion and unnecessary sexuality into their childhood experience that could have been (and should have been) as simple as possible, for as long as possible. And I would ward off the iconic toys that tyrannized our household for years.

When did the invasion begin? So long ago. Just when I thought I had succeeded in insulating my two young daughters pretty successfully from certain trendy toddler favorites, my older daughter, Lucy, asked me to buy her a "Barbecue doll." She was four. I had been so careful, running the Care Bear, Strawberry Shortcake, Hello Kitty, Smurf, Cabbage Patch gauntlet (this was 1985), but I had somehow been ambushed by Ken's perennial prom date. "I really want an inappropriate doll," she implored.

I was taken aback. This had come much sooner than I remembered from my own childhood. What was next, puberty at seven? We had already begun to discuss where babies came from, although the first time I explained it all to Lucy, in as clear and simple and enlightened a way as I could, and she seemed to get it, and I asked her if she had any questions, she had just one solemn inquiry: Do other people know about this?

But now she wanted a Barbie. I had absolutely no nostalgic affection for Barbie, none whatsoever, because I had not played with Barbie dolls. I had grown up with friends who lavished all sorts of attention on their Barbies, but I was never compelled by those long blond tresses, or by all the wardrobe options, the accessories, the plastic cars and cardboard dwellings, the plastic friends, the intriguingly smooth-crotched boyfriend.

But I didn't want to impose my own childhood peculiarities on my daughters. That had been done to me, by a mother who had often seemed far more interested in her own childhood experiences than in mine. I knew what it was like to have my mother's preferences in toys and books and games be my preferences, no questions asked. As a matter of fact, that is probably why I wasn't a Barbie kind of girl—I was a weird kid playing on my own, too immersed in my mother's Big Little Books, too busy gingerly handling my mother's stuffed animals from 1927.

And so, somehow, it made sense for a Malibu Barbie to come into our life. I treated her coldly, I confess. I wasn't downright rude, just minimally polite. The way you might be to your first husband's second wife, say.

"Don't you just love her hair, Mommy?" Lucy would ask, thrusting Barbie my way by the feet, the way you hand someone a pair of scissors.

"Not especially," I would answer, trying to walk the occasionally thin line between veracity and unkindness toward one's child.

But then the thrill wore off. Lucy's younger sister, Charlotte, scribbled on her with a surprisingly indelible pink marker. Barbie wasn't cuddly and so was rarely accorded bedroom privileges. She was even left outside overnight a few times. Her shoes—slutty little pink sling backs—got lost. Her hair was a snarled tangle, a chunk in the back partly hacked off under mysterious circumstances. Her single garment—Lucy, at four, had somehow never cottoned to the whole true purpose of Barbie's existence as an excuse to buy garments and accessories, and I certainly wasn't going to be the one to point this out—became pilled and grubby. The elastic on this short pink dress wore out, causing the top to slip down over one "breast" most of the time. Malibu Barbie had developed a peculiar, haggard, sort of crack-whore look.

Having never been a thrill, now she was a disaster. Without her shoes, Barbie had no ability to stand up, because her feet were formed in that weird, permanent tiptoes arch, suitable only for teetering around on high heels. (Surely, Barbie has atrophied little plastic Achilles tendons.) Nobody liked her anymore.

Was it small of me to be so unwelcoming to a plastic doll? Barbie felt like the enemy. She was a mass of points and hair. She had insanely thin thighs and the fixed, vapid smile of someone taking way too much Xanax. How could my toddler find emotional nourishment and positive identification from this? I was relieved at Barbie's downfall, and yet I felt mildly guilty. But in the end I thought we had dodged that bullet so successfully, worked it through, let it play out . . .

Then came the My Little Ponies. Then came, in fact, an entire decade of rainbows and unicorns. Translucent rubber bracelets. An endless series of cute, rubbery, pastel objects cascaded through our household. It was the herald of an alarming cultural trend that has lasted from then to now, the gummification of America. There was a time, before this era, when a small child could tell right away if an object was meant to be eaten, worn, or played with, but those boundaries became hopelessly blurred in the mid-eighties. But now Gummy Bears looked like creepy rubber Halloween worms and spiders, which looked like rubber jewelry, which looked like gummy snakes, rats, fish, pacifiers, which looked like gummy, translucent erasers impregnated with the smell of Lifesavers candy. (Lifesavers candy is now available with a gummy option, too.) All of it looked like material you would once have found only in the bait bins at a tackle shop.

Were the seeds for all this gumminess sown in my own childhood, with Gumby, that first mass-produced gummy toy? Remember his orange horse, Pokey? The Claymation Gumby television show used to creep me out. I hated Gumby. I hated his voice, which sounded like a woman's, and I loathed his sweetness, and I was bothered by his strange rhomboid head. There was something nightmarish about him altogether. He seemed like something left over from some era that never was. But then, unlike my daughters, who from preschool were always acutely attuned and aware of the latest fashions and trends, whether or not they joined them, I was not in the swim of things. This was why I eschewed Trolls.

If you're a female between the ages of, say, forty-five and fifty-five, you remember Trolls. They were really ugly, naked creatures with pot bellies and no genitalia, with hideous big tufts of neon and pastel hair. They looked a lot like Don King, actually (though I have never seen him naked, and I assume he does have genitals). They came in a variety of colors and sizes. Their hair was the key to their success. Little girls like to comb hair. Little girls *love* to comb hair.

Most of my friends combed their trolls compulsively. Underneath desks at study halls, during current events, the furtive troll-combings took place all around me. (I preferred to rub my pink eraser on the bronze inkwell cover on my desk, and then hoard the velvety pile of eraser crumbs in my pencil trough.

But I was, as previously noted, an oddball, a loner.) All of this activity was undoubtedly sublimation for other sorts of activities that were not encouraged in elementary school classrooms. And the faddishness of them made them somehow acceptable. I believe that you can draw a direct line, a pink and purple gummy line, from the Trolls of the sixties, which were second only to Barbie in sales, to the My Little Pony phenomenon in the eighties. But even the Troll-obsessed had only a few. A collection of a dozen was impressive. That was the sixties. This was the eighties.

My Little Ponies soon infested our house. They had pastel manes and tails, in contrasting colors to their pink and purple and green and blue and yellow bodies. I am ashamed to say how many we probably had under our roof at the peak of the obsession. Possibly a couple of hundred. I am pretty sure some of them had been stolen from other children, just as some ours in turn were stolen by other children. To have My Little Pony was to be obsessed by My Little Pony, to be possessed by insatiable greed and desire to amass more My Little Ponies. They traveled with us in the car. There were Ponies in almost every room in the house. No one Pony had particular charm or character. What they lacked in individuality—everything—they made up for in sheer quantity. It was like a curse—to possess a My Little Pony was to want another, and another, although getting *enough* My Little Ponies was an impossibility, like trying to fill a bucket with a hole in the bottom. Then we got the Dreamcastle. It took up the middle of the playroom, displacing some very nice wooden blocks from Sweden. It somewhat resembled a small and elaborate beaver den, in bulk, though this thing had plastic drawbridges and turrets, and it did not look like something one could find in nature anywhere on this earth. Only representative Ponies lived there, as it was too small to contain them all.

I crossed a line of some kind when I agreed to take Lucy and Charlotte to see *My Little Pony—The Movie* one spring afternoon. They were only four and five, and it was more important to them that they see it, and they really wanted to see it, than it was important to me that we *not* see it. You pick your battles. Off we went to the movie complex. Fortified with—what else?—Gummy Bears and Gummy Worms, we sat through a terrible ninety minutes about an evil witch who was sending "the smooze," a living pastel purple slime, to obliterate the cutesy pastel land of the Ponies, where they sang second-rate jingles and romped around their Dreamcastle (so much bigger and better than the one at home that Lucy and Charlotte were now doomed to be disappointed forever with ours, after this one viewing of the "real" Dreamcastle). Perhaps "the smooze" was not intended as a metaphor for Communism. I am sure I got a lot more out of this movie than I was meant to, because there was not much content, though it did invite a certain kind of postmodern deconstruction, and perhaps it offered some otherwise hidden dimension of meaning to people taking hallucinogens.

Despite the relentlessly lisping sweetness, the movie was actually filled with violence. I watched my daughters watching the screen avidly. I longed for real characters and story, for the sharply defined populace of Beatrix Potter books. Why were we here on this sunny afternoon? I was suddenly ashamed at my laziness, at my willingness for my family to be swept along on this pastel tide of smarm. We left the theater cranky and unfulfilled, though my daughters claimed to have loved every minute. They fought in the car. When we got home, I picked a fight with my husband.

That was twenty years ago, and I'm clearly not over it yet. Were My Little Ponies really so bad?

I say, yes, they really were. From the aesthetic, so to speak, of My Little Ponies, it was a short hop to the "beauty"-themed slumber party from which my daughters, at seven and nine, emerged with glued-on rhinestones and airbrushed flowers on their nails that had been done by "real manicurists from a salon!" Why was I the only parent at pick-up who didn't think this was great?

The girls seemed to feel they should dress for My Little Pony World for several years. Every item of clothing was ideally pink or purple, with bonus points for fluff and sequins. But then they mutated. At nine and eleven, my daughters seemed destined to be Vegas showgirls. Could this have been farther from my own unadorned style, which featured blue jeans and old sweaters? Was it that simple—they were rejecting me and my values? When did Cher's personal style become a personal goal for my little girls? But maybe it had nothing at all to do with me.

Maybe it was just what was out there. There was a kind of cheapness, a certain kind of pre-slut look, which they both mastered without fully comprehending what it was. Accessories and clothing weren't even really necessary for it to happen—it was a certain kind of body language, a sulky, sultry, slinky projection of themselves as models, as famous women on display in the public eye. They were both capable of switching this on at certain disconcerting moments, though they were both equally capable of being happy latent children, playing softball, riding their bikes in old shorts and T-shirts, poking sticks in puddles.

It's one thing to ban makeup or to forbid certain clothing, but it's much harder to tell your child she shouldn't walk with that hip-sway or tilt her head a certain way that was surely studied in magazines and on television—a pseudo-sexy come-hither, pouty liquid movement of the neck that played at a kind of womanliness they didn't understand. Why did we, the parents, tolerate it to the extent that we did? Why was the first long, lingering, clearly sexual once-over beamed at one of my daughters, aged ten, by a grown-up man in a coffee shop, not sufficiently creepy to compel me to slam the brakes on the whole thing? Because there was no single big moment. There were thousands of small moments that didn't feel quite right all adding up. At that time, I didn't really understand, or couldn't afford to acknowledge, emotionally, what was going on. It's all so much clearer in hindsight.

The inculcated greed of My Little Pony–owning was, I believe, even more insidious than the aesthetic junkiness. It signaled a kind of cultural approval for being insatiable; it was a celebration of getting and spending. Where do you go from My Little Pony? It's the ideal conditioning for a little girl to grow up and become a compulsive shopper. Spending and eating disorders are of course very connected, both being about taking in more than you need or want. A very wise woman I know once said to me, "You never get enough of what you don't really want," and it's true.

I won't invade my daughters' privacy by detailing of the angst of their darker adolescent moments. That would be something pretty imperfect and regrettable for me to do, as a mother who is still trying to get it right. Suffice it to say we have all come out the other side. I am sure if either of them were asked to write an essay for a collection called *The Imperfect Mom* they would have a lot of material.

We had a huge tag sale when Lucy and Charlotte were thirteen and fifteen. They sold every single My Little Pony, every last one. They cleared $75. Did Charlotte want to hold on to just one or two, for sentimental reasons, I wondered? No, she told me, she had never really liked them, had never given them names. The urgency that surrounded the accumulation of the My Little Ponies was most of their appeal. Lucy had no interest either. Neither of them could explain why she had ever really liked them without referring to other girls who had possessed even more Ponies. We got twenty bucks for the Dreamcastle.

Rochelle Jewel Shapiro

~~~~~~

My father always wanted a son. Instead, he was stuck with two daughters and a wife who didn't want to become pregnant again.

In despair, he took my mother to Madame Krinsky, a local tea leaf reader who was famous in Rockaway Beach, Queens, for the accuracy of her predictions—she had even predicted World War II.

Madame Krinksy, her face like a dried apple doll with false eyelashes, looked up from her cup. "Vait five years and you vill have a boy," she prophesied.

My mother was more than happy to wait. With each pregnancy, it had been harder to get her figure back. She would rather have been a size eight again than have a son. But in 1947, when the five years were up, she went along with my father's wishes, and it paid off. My father began bringing her flowers and boxes of chocolate as he had when they were courting. He made her cups of peppermint tea to settle her stomach and massaged her swollen feet.

Even though my Russian father was superstitious about buying anything for an unborn child, he couldn't resist a pair of miniature boxing gloves for his future son, and because he wanted him to be a real American, he brought home a tiny baseball and a pint-sized bat.

During my mother's labor, every time a nurse appeared, he'd grab her arm and ask, "So, is my son here yet?"

Four hours later, the doctor proudly announced, "It's a girl."

My father couldn't answer. He lost his voice for six weeks and patches of his beard fell out. He couldn't even look at my mother. In turn, my mother couldn't look at me. Instead of nursing me as she had my sisters, she fed me bottles of Carnation evaporated milk. As soon as I could crawl, she stuck me in a playpen in front of the TV. When I was five, she went to work in my father's grocery store six days a week from early in the morning until well after dark and left me in the care of a woman who watched TV along with me and never spoke. Her only sound was the swishing of lime Jell-O between her teeth.

My father felt lost in his family of women. On Sundays, he wouldn't join us at the beach or for walks on the boardwalk or at a movie anymore. He'd stay home and sleep too many hours, and drink too much seltzer, and put his hand to his heart and belch.

"I've got to have a son to say Kaddish for me someday," he told my mother.

My mother was worried that he'd need the prayer for the dead said for him sooner rather than later if he didn't cheer up.

"Let's try again," she said.

This time, she consulted a ladies' magazine that suggested douching with a solution of warm vinegar-water before sex would increase the chances of having a boy.

When I was eight, she became pregnant. My sisters, one already sixteen, the other thirteen, were embarrassed and stayed away from home—and from me—as much as possible. I, though, was intrigued. A living doll, I thought.

When my brother was born, my parents called him "The Messiah." It was chocolate and roses all over again for my mother. And it was only the best for my brother, too. Not only did my parents enroll him in private school, but they bought him every toy on TV. Transistor radios were fairly new then. My father, knowing nothing about batteries, bought him a new radio each time one stopped playing.

My brother had such a crinkle-up-his-face smile and a hic-cupy laugh, that soon my sisters and I loved him as much as my parents did. Having a baby at forty-two made my mother feel as young as her new diet-pill figure. But while my father and my mother couldn't stop talking about their son, we girls might have been invisible.

One day, when I was sixteen and helping out at my father's grocery, a customer asked him what grade I was in. I was proudly waiting for my father to tell him that I was a junior, an honors student, and that I'd won an award for French.

My father shrugged. "All I know is I'm saving up for her wedding. The sooner a girl is married off, the better," and he and the customer began to laugh. My father might have been joking, but it was no joke to me. I felt like produce that cost him money and that he'd have to throw away if it wasn't sold in time. At that moment, my father made me a feminist. I swore that if I had a daughter, and I hoped I would, I'd honor and value her as a girl, and I made sure before I married that my husband agreed with me.

When I became pregnant, and my father said, "I hope it's a

boy," I became enraged with him and stayed away. He died six weeks before my daughter was born.

At the gravesite, I forgave him for his prejudices from the shtetl. He would never have a chance to learn to love my daughter—or disapprove of her—but I would make it all up to her.

I would never leave her alone the way I had been. Even though my back was aching, I wore her in a baby snuggler as I vacuumed, did the laundry, went for walks.

"Put her down!" my mother would tell me, but how could I believe the woman who stuck me in a playpen and turned her back?

When I ate a meal, I propped my daughter before me in an infant seat on the table and gazed at her adoringly. I never grew tired of looking into her big brown eyes, patting the strawberry blond curls that only grew on the top of her head. I was even fascinated by the bubble of drool that hung suspended from her chin. She became bigger than life to me. Whenever I looked at one of the thousands of photos my husband and I took of her, I couldn't believe how small she actually was.

Nights, I tiptoed into her bedroom. By the dim glow of the nightlight, I watched her eyelids fluttering and her lips dream-sucking. If she made a peep, I'd take her up in my arms and walk the house with her, singing her lullabies, patting her tiny back. In the morning, I was always at her crib, waiting for her eyelids to open.

"Good morning, Sunshine," I'd sing and her face would bloom into a smile and her legs pedaled as if she were cycling into my arms.

After what I'd been through in childhood, I didn't even own

a playpen. I spent hours with my daughter in my lap, singing her songs, reading her books, playing this-little-piggy.

From the get-go, I wanted my daughter to know that her education meant as much as any boy's. While she was still in diapers, I took her to MoMA, the Whitney, and the Metropolitan. In those days, strollers weren't allowed in museums, so I carried her for hours in a backpack. She weighed a lot more than she had in her "snuggler days." My shoulders shrieked with pain, but that didn't stop me. I was her docent, explaining the "simultaneity" of Cubist art, Morris Louis's technique of pouring paint onto unprimed canvas. I told her about the Egyptian sun god, Akenatun, and his wife, Nefertiti.

"Bah," she'd say, clapping my head with her little hands, and kicking my sides with her white baby shoes as if she were a jockey spurring me on.

Even when we took regular walks, she in the stroller or toddling beside me, I narrated everything we passed. "That's an elm tree," I'd say. "That's a basset hound and look over there. A dalmation!"

By the time she was three, we were making clay figurines, papier-mâché piñatas, and building Lego towers. We made tape recordings of stories she told me and we wrote poems together.

"Give her some breathing space," my husband said.

"No, no, this is just what she needs," I insisted.

One day, when I went into our own bathroom without her, she sobbed at the closed door. When I came out, I found her lying on the floor, spent and exhausted. Later, when we were going outside, she clung to me, terrified. I had to put on her coat first so she wouldn't think I was going to leave her. She was almost four by then, too old for that kind of behavior. Instead of making her feel important as I'd hoped, I had made her afraid to be alone. She couldn't sleep unless I sat by her bed and held her hand until she drifted off.

Why had this happened? I began to think back. Yes, I had been left alone, but in the aloneness, I had learned to play records on my Victrola by myself. "In the land of France, a little girl named Tina loved to dance, dance, dance, and they called her ballerina." I finger painted. I pretended I could read books by describing the pictures to myself. I made faces in front of the mirror and set my doll's hair with Jo-Cur lotion. Sometimes, I'd wake up screaming from a recurrent dream of a wild dog chasing me.

"Shut up!" my father yelled, and I'd pop my thumb into my mouth and go right to sleep.

I realized that for my daughter's own good, I had to wean her from my constant presence. I had to give her the "breathing space" my husband had been suggesting. I had to harden my heart to her tears.

It took many years to undo the damage I'd done. I got her into a playgroup where she bawled almost the whole time. And so did I! I sat in my car, resisting going in after her, telling myself this was for the best. As she got older, I sent her to sleep-away camps where she could never fall asleep.

In her junior year of high school, I sent her on a Wilderness Expedition where she hiked across states, kayaked across rivers, and dug her own latrines. When I picked her up at the airport, for the first time, I noticed something good had happened. She strode toward me, her hiking boots mud-caked, her knees scraped from climbing mountains, her brown curls wild, her eyes bright, her face and whole bearing full of confidence.

Today, she's a powerful woman about to have her own child.

She pulls up her shirt to proudly show me how big her stomach has gotten. She takes my hand and presses it against her belly. Neither of us cares whether her baby will be a boy or a girl. All we care about is the miraculous, independent thump of the kick.

Julie Aigner-Clark

I looked at my daughters today, and I wondered where the time went. That time I'd wished away. Can't wait till she can walk; can't wait till they can play together; can't wait till she sleeps through the night. Can't wait till they go to school. They're in school, now, and the house is empty. But for me. Here. Afternoon shadows making ghosts of those little girls in little pajamas with rubber-soled feet.

I remember big events, births and birthday parties, growth charts and hospital visits, trips full of photographs. But the times that I meant to remember are gone. The way her face looked when she rode a two-wheeler for the first time. The soft stillness of their warm skin as they slept, one surrounded by thirty-four stuffed animals, the other breathing softly, thumb between six tiny teeth. The expression on my older daughter's face when she popped a jalapeño pepper in her mouth, thinking it was a piece of chocolate. The seriousness with which my younger child played Peter Pan and fought an invisible Captain Hook with a plastic sword.

I watched my daughters leave for school this morning and felt the tug of wishing, wishing they were little again. The older one, so grown-up now, curled hair and flared jeans. And my younger child, scooping up her backpack and lunch. There was a brief exchange, a kiss on the cheek from one and a wave from another, and they were gone.

There was a time when I heard "Mommy?" at least one hundred times a day. How I'd wished for silence. Now I am the one asking questions, begging, almost, for scraps of information about their day: How was school? What made you laugh? What made you cry? Who is that boy? What is the name of the girl who pushed you on the playground?

There was a time when I knew every minute of every hour of every day what was happening in their lives, and it made me tired. How I long to be tired like that again.

My children have people, new and different people, separate and apart from me. I knew this would happen but I didn't realize what it would feel like. I am so proud. I am so . . . what? Melancholy. Curious. I look at these children and don't know any longer just what is going on inside of them as I did when they nursed at my breast or cried in frustration or needed a diaper changed. Now there's the daughter who competes in karate and spars against boys when her mom can scarcely throw a punch. There's the daughter who plays violin and can figure out any computer game, while I can't carry a tune or find my way around a word processing program. They are in some ways strangers to me now. How strange.

I have had an amazing life. I have grown up with loving parents, studied what I wanted to in college, married a remarkable man. I have run a multimillion dollar business and created an entirely new market segment that I'm proud of, one that exposes little kids to great works of art. I have survived breast cancer with a strength I didn't know I had. I have made great friends and met fascinating people. And yet the most amazing thing that I have done is to have had children. I know this is something that most women do sometime in their lives, and while it's something that's not unique or unusual in any way, I still view it as my most fulfilling life's work.

So why did I wish it away? Because I was tired? Because I wanted to go out to dinner and not carry a baby seat or cut someone else's food or hurry through my meal? Because I wanted to sleep later or longer or better?

I have time, now. I can sleep all day. But I'm no longer deliciously, deliriously, satisfyingly tired.

Lorraine Glennon

The list of my "imperfections" (quite a euphemism, that) as a mother is both lengthy and entirely ordinary, running the gamut from screaming at my children to saying hurtful things (including, naturally, many of the choice phrases my mother used to hurl at me and which I vowed never to utter to my own children) to giving them the occasional swat. But when I consider these maternal crimes, what emerges most clearly is that they were all unpremeditated—occasions of sin into which I fell unwittingly, blinded by my rage of the moment (and about which, of course, I felt horribly abject afterward). That's why it galls me to acknowledge that one of my biggest blunders as a mother is one I walked into with my eyes wide open: I very deliberately absolved my children of the need to perform any household chores.

Why on earth would anyone do that, you might well ask. Why indeed? I had my reasons. As a child and especially as a teenager, I was oppressed by all the work I had to do around the house. I was the second child of four, but the oldest girl, which—despite my mother's later passionate embrace of feminism—meant that I got saddled with taking care of the younger kids, cleaning up the kitchen after school, doing laundry and hanging the clothes out on the clothesline (a job I particularly *loathed*), starting nightly dinner and then doing dinner dishes every other night (the one chore that my older brother alternated with me). For performing all these tasks, I received not a dime beyond my modest weekly allowance.

I recognize now just how beleaguered my mother felt and just what an uphill a battle it was to run a six-person household. Imagine coming home from your full-time job and preparing a full-course, hot dinner for that many people every single night, including weekends (yes, my father expected it and no, we never went out or ordered in, *ever*). The amount of sheer labor involved is mind-boggling, and in retrospect I sympathize with my mother's plight and salute her efforts.

At the time, though, the only emotion I could muster about all my domestic duties was pure, distilled resentment. And, in my own defense, I wasn't the only one who thought I was overburdened. Even now, my cousin (who was my closest friend in high school) remarks on the inordinate amount of housework I had to do as a teenager, and remembers how I could never hang out with her and our other friends after school because I always had to rush home to clean up the kitchen and start dinner before my mom got back from work.

Today, from the vantage point of adulthood, I do not believe that any of this instilled discipline, taught me responsibility, strengthened my character, or provided any of the other benefits that are commonly said to derive from such drudgery. Nope. I just hated it. All of it. Indeed, I'm convinced that, if anything, all this housework at an early age helped turn me into a slob for a good part of my adult life. (Once, as a graduate student, I actually moved dirty dishes from my old apartment to my new.) The realization that I *didn't have to do this anymore* filled me with an almost-giddy excitement, and I went on strike virtually for years. What liberation. (What chaos.)

So you can see why I made the decision I did when I became a mother myself. I had hated doing chores, ergo, I would spare my children the same pain. The all-too-predictable result, of course, has been that my daughter and son (who both show formidable work ethics when it comes to, say, writing political screeds or practicing basketball, to name two of their favorite pastimes) are generally helpless around the house and expect me and my husband to wait on them hand and foot. When there's a blizzard, is it our able-bodied seventeen-year-old who's out on the sidewalk clearing away the snow? No, that would be my fifty-something husband wielding the shovel, courting a heart attack. When I stagger in with five bags of groceries, does either child greet me in the kitchen and start putting the food away? What a hilarious concept.

But it gets worse. On some level, I *enjoy* doing everything for them. It's a bit of a sickness that even my son has noticed. "You really like waiting on me, don't you?" he'll ask semi-jokingly, as I scurry around making his breakfast while he sits scanning the Sports page. The truth is, yes, I do. Call it working-mom guilt. Call it overcompensation or a martyr complex. But in my home, I'm the queen of servitude.

Still, even I have my limits. Perhaps the nadir was one day when my son was around twelve and hence able to stay by himself while I went out. As I was walking out the door, he asked if there was any food in the house for him to eat. I suggested that if he got hungry, he could simply open a can of soup. "I can't do that," he said with perfect equanimity, "I don't know how to work a can opener."

It was what *Ms.* magazine used to call a "click" moment. *My twelve-year-old doesn't know how to work a can opener?* It was a sobering moment—what had I wrought?—and I vowed to reverse the trend. I could not let this ineptitude and sloth continue, I chastised myself. I was doing my children a grave disservice by letting them slog into adulthood lacking survival skills as basic as being able to operate a common kitchen utensil. And wouldn't they curse me one day when they woke up at, say, twenty and realized they couldn't sew on a button or make a pot of coffee because their mother had never taught them?

But as every parent knows, it's nearly always more work to get others to help than to continue doing the work yourself. (That those others are banking on your feeling this way doesn't alter the basic fact.) Oh, I made a few halfhearted efforts to toughen up—I distinctly remember printing out a list of chores and posting it on the refrigerator, along with a strip of smiley-face stickers that (in theory) would be peeled off and affixed next to each successfully completed task—but recidivism was inevitable, and almost instant. In the end, I am embarrassed to say, I simply threw in the towel. My efforts to rehabilitate my children were a case of too little, too late; I simply could not summon the stamina to see it through. That is why I always urge new parents to get their kids doing chores early and often—in other words, while they're still young and misguided enough to believe that helping Mom and Dad with housework is *fun.* That way, when they're older and have caught on to the fact that fun it ain't, they'll already have been indoctrinated to believe that performing chores is an inescapable part of being a fully functioning member of a household.

On the other hand, maybe I'm as behind in the times on this subject as my kids tell me I am on most others. Certainly, there's mounting evidence that the rest of society is catching up to them. Have you checked out soup cans lately? They now come equipped with pop-tabs, just like soda or beer, for the can-opener-impaired. "See, Mom?" I can hear my son saying. "All your fears were groundless." And in fact, chores or no chores, both my children seem to be turning into remarkable people, possessing not only a sweet and generous spirit toward others but also the coveted ability to perform well on standardized tests. (What more, really, could a modern mother ask for?)

So I choose to view the obsolescence of can openers as a vindication of my child-rearing methods. Indeed, I see now that in exempting my children from household duties, I imparted a much more vital life lesson than could ever be learned from pushing a broom or emptying a trash can: if you hold out long enough, kids, the world will eventually come around.

CELEBRATING IMPERFECTION: CONFESSIONS OF A HIGHLY SUSPECT MOTHER

Suzanne Finnamore

~~~~~~

I tell you this: No eternal reward will forgive us now for wasting the dawn.

—JIM MORRISON

Dawn is never wasted at our house. My son, Pablo, a hale seven-year-old who looks remarkably like Marlon Brando in *On the Waterfront*, is a morning person. He and I live together in a small house in Marin County, home of the $29.95 appetizer. We eat out very infrequently. We save up for a five-dollar mango. It's obscenely expensive here; it is also beautiful and rich with culture. So we stay. I decided to stay, in that magical period where one's child has no vote whatsoever. They can't even raise their hands properly. It was a brief time, but I do remember it with certain nostalgia. Now I have to negotiate every trip from our home to anywhere at any time. I have to find reasons for moving, good ones, or else Pablo gets out the hammer and nails his metaphorical shoes to the floor.

I used to be a morning person, when morning meant 9:00 a.m. and not the first crack of light as it comes over the San

Francisco bay horizon. There is a goodly three- or four-hour gap between my son's morning and my old morning. I was the one to adjust. I am usually the one to adjust, but I am not always the one to adjust. This makes me highly imperfect, as a mother. As a wife, it made me untenable to Pablo's father, who now lives in another state and just visits. We have an amicable divorce, which means that everyone is still alive.

It's frightening to think that you mark your children merely by being yourself. . . . It seems unfair. You can't assume the responsibility for everything you do—or don't do.
— SIMONE DE BEAUVOIR, *LES BELLES IMAGE*

I would like to tell you all the terrible, wrong, and politically incorrect acts I have performed as a mother, but you couldn't handle that. (I know I couldn't. Plus, then it would be in writing, never a good idea when sweeping mistakes are concerned.) So I will only allude to the lightest of my sins and leave the larger travesties of justice to my son's future therapist, a woman who may have yet to be born. I hope she is Jungian and I hope she is reasonable.

Here's one example: I've been home all week without Pablo, who is at his grandparents' house, a scant forty miles away.

When people ask me if I miss him, I say, "No."

Then they laugh and say, "Oh I know you do!"

But I really don't, unless someone starts talking about him (my friends know not to) or I do something perverse, like whip out his baby book while he is forty miles away. In fact, not only do I not miss him, I feel incredible. I could run around the block ten times. Instead, as the sun creeps into the West, I will pour an icy glass of wine and watch *Entertainment Tonight* and *The Insider* and *Dr. Phil*: all of which I had the foresight to tape last night while I was in San Francisco falling down laughing at my friend's birthday party. This is something mothers are not supposed to do: fall down laughing, especially in public and not at an amusement park.

Since people are going to be living longer and getting older, they'll just have to learn how to be babies longer.

— ANDY WARHOL

Yes. I'd dolled myself up and went to my friend Ken's fortieth birthday party at the Clift Hotel in San Francisco (designed by Ian Schrager, who could have had a place in the Gestapo, so severe and perfect are his forms and lines). Ken had nicked a penthouse suite from the front desk; the gay mafia was involved, he paid something like $100 for the whole night and it was 900 square feet. Everyone I love was there (except my son and my parents), there was a pitcher of Cosmopolitans and a crazy bald man who kept running around refilling drinks while no one was looking so everyone thought they had one drink and really they had ten or twelve. Toward the end of the evening, I sat in the 3X scale Louis Quatorze chair in the lobby, like a sassy doll on a highchair, and I shouted across the lobby to my friends and they took pictures of me and shouted back. We cleared the lobby within minutes and took right over. Mothers do not clear lobbies, unless their child has gone missing and they are hysterical. I was hysterical, but not with fear: with joy and mirth. This is decidedly unmotherly, especially when you are not laughing at something amazing your precocious child has just said, you are laughing at a joke that a drag queen has just made involving a false-bottom vase and a succulent plant.

The party was so good I fell down on the floor laughing. Twice. Once on the balcony, and once in the elevator going down on the way out with two semi-famous designers, when we mistakenly took the service elevator and ended up in some horrible industrial yellow place in the bowels of the hotel, where a dwarf with a stiff white hat yelled at us. Yes, the whole carefully constructed aesthetic of the evening was ruined, which struck us all as unbearably funny and it's amazing we made it out of the hotel at all, so crippled we were with irrational mirth.

Work is X, Y is Play, and Z is keeping your mouth shut.
—ALBERT EINSTEIN

Upon his arrival back home, Pablo says that a leprechaun jumped into my parents' bathroom window last night.

"Do you believe in leprechauns?" he asks me.

"Oh yes certainly. I believe in all magic . . ." I say brightly.

"You can't believe in everything." Pablo says, deadpan. Then he turns around and shuffles down the hallway in his wide-wale corduroy pants, *swoosh swoosh swoosh*. He's gotten me again. I laugh, and way down the stairway I can hear him laughing too.

This is all that matters. Those other things don't matter. The things I didn't tell you don't matter either, because they are a secret. I'm free and I'm a mother. I love my son more than life, but I will not give him my life like a subway token to do with as he pleases. I think it's fair, but whether it's fair or not is irrelevant, because I am the mother.

Good-bye. May you take a moment for yourself today, and

may you stretch it into several hours. May you put yourself first occasionally, and may you fall down laughing very soon. I wish you well, and I wish your children well. My child and I are very happy. That too is somewhat suspect: I am batting 1,000.

SHANA ABORN, formerly a senior editor at *Ladies' Home Journal*, is currently a contributing editor at *Redbook* and a writer for such magazines as *Parents*, *Working Mother*, and *Organic Style*. Her book, *30 Days to a More Spiritual Life*, was published by Doubleday in 2000. She and her husband live in New York City with their son, Daniel, and daughter, Sarah.

JULIE AIGNER-CLARK founded the Baby Einstein Company, a billion-dollar media industry centered on stimulating the minds of infants and toddlers. A recipient of Ernst and Young's Entrepreneur of the Year Award, *Working Mother*'s Entrepreneur of the Year Award, and Michigan State University's Distinguished Alumni Award, she is president of Aigner-Clark Creative, which combines her love of the creative process with her commitment to charitable giving.

GAIL BELSKY is an editorial consultant. She is the former executive editor of Time, Inc., Custom Publishing Division, and *Working Mother* magazine, and was an editor with *Parents* magazine.

NANCY BILYEAU is an articles editor at *Ladies' Home Journal*. She has worked as a staff editor at *Good Housekeeping*, *Rolling Stone*, *Mademoiselle*, and *American Film*. She is also a screenwriter; her new script, *Sweet Love in Despair*, has won quarterfinalist or finalist status in four national contests. She and her husband, Max, have two children, Alexander and Nora.

KATHRYN BLACK is the author of the bestselling *Mothering Without a Map: The Search for the Good Mother Within* (Viking, 2004), which received a general nonfiction award from the American Society of Journalists and Authors, and *In the Shadow of Polio*, named by the *Boston Globe* as one of the ten best 1996 nonfiction works, and winner of the Colorado Book Award for Literary Nonfiction and the June Roth Book Award for Health and Medical Writing. Black, who was named 1997 Author of the Year by the American Society of Journalists and Authors, has written for many national magazines. She lives in Boulder, Colorado.

GAYLE BRANDEIS is the author of *Fruitflesh: Seeds of Inspiration for Women Who Write*, *Dictionary Poems*, and *The Book of Dead Birds*, which won the 2002 Bellwether Prize in Support of a Literature of Social Change established by Barbara Kingsolver. Gayle's poetry, fiction, and essays have appeared in numerous magazines and anthologies, such as *Salon, hip Mama*, and *Brain, Child*, and have received several awards, including the QPB/Story Magazine Short Story Award and a grant from the Barbara Deming Memorial Fund. She was named a 2004 Writer Who Makes a Difference by *The Writer Magazine*, and lives in Riverside, California, with her husband and two children.

ANDREA J. BUCHANAN is the author of the bestselling *Mother Shock: Loving Every (Other) Minute of It* (Seal Press, 2003), and is managing editor of LiteraryMama.com, an online literary magazine for the maternally inclined. Her work has been featured in the *Christian Science Monitor*, *Parents*, and *Nick Jr.* magazines; in the collection *Breeder: Real Life Stories from the New Generation of Mothers*; and in online parenting magazines such as PregnancyandBaby.com and hipMama.com. She is the editor of three anthologies forthcoming from Seal Press: *It's A Boy: Women Writers on Raising Sons* (October 2005), *Literary Mama: Writing from the Literary Magazine for the Maternally Inclined* (January 2006), and *It's A Girl: Women Writers on Raising Daughters* (April 2006).

DEBORAH CALDWELL is a senior editor and national correspondent at Beliefnet, where she specializes in matters of religion and spirituality. Previously, she was a senior writer at the *Dallas Morning News*. Her work has also appeared in the *New York Times* and *Slate*, and she is a contributor to two books on religion in America. She has been interviewed on ABC News, CNN, National Public Radio, the Hallmark Channel, and Oxygen television, and for numerous print publications. She lives with her two sons in the blissful suburbs of New Jersey.

JESSICA CARLSON cocreated the popular Web site the Imperfect Parent (imperfectparent.com) with her husband in 2002. She is the mother of two boys.

TRISH DALTON is a senior editor at a major New York publishing house. She's married and the mother of two children.

GABRIELLE ERICKSON is a pseudonym for a freelance writer living in New Jersey.

SUZANNE FINNAMORE, bestselling author of the novels *The Zygote Chronicles* and *Otherwise Engaged*, is a columnist for *Child* magazine, and a frequent contributor to O magazine and Salon.com. She lives with her son in Northern California.

MARGOT GILMAN is the deputy editor of *Ladies' Home Journal*. Previously, she was the editor-in-chief of *Know-How* magazine, and was a senior editor at *Psychology Today*. Her work has appeared in *McCall's, Family Circle, Seventeen,* and *Reader's Digest*. She lives in New York City with her husband and two daughters, Thea and Lily.

LORRAINE GLENNON is articles editor at *Ladies' Home Journal*. She lives in Brooklyn with her husband and two almost-grown children, Claire and Thomas. The former features editor at *Parents* magazine, she was the editor-in-chief of *Our Times*, a one-volume illustrated history of the twentieth century, and has also edited three other books, including *Those Who Can . . . Teach!* and *Those Who Can . . . Coach!*

AYUN HALLIDAY is the sole staff member of the quarterly zine *The East Village Inky*, and the author of *The Big Rumpus: A Mother's Tale from the Trenches, No Touch Monkey! And Other Travelers' Lessons Learned Too Late,* and *Job Hopper*. She is *BUST* magazine's Mother Superior columnist and also contributes to NPR, *hip Mama*, and more anthologies than you can shake a stick at without dangling a participle. A Hoosier

New Yorker, she lives with her husband and well-documented children in a very small apartment in Brooklyn, where she's allegedly hard at work on a memoir to be published in the spring of ought-six, *Dirty Sugar Cookies: Culinary Observations, Questionable Taste.*

LU HANESSIAN is the author of *Let the Baby Drive: Navigating the Road of New Motherhood* (St. Martin's Press, 2004), and the host of "Make Room for Baby" and "Total Family Health" on Discovery Health Channel. Her essays and articles have been published in the *New York Times*, *Redbook*, *Mothering*, *Parenting*, and *Fit Pregnancy*, to which she is a contributing writer. She, her husband, and their two boys, six and three, live in New Jersey. She is currently working on a book about intuitive parenting.

KELLY HARRINGTON JOHNSON is a former attorney turned freelance writer. She lives in Richmond, Virginia, with her husband, their four children, two wonderful stepsons, and one impossibly old cat.

KATE KELLY is the managing editor of *American Baby*, to which she is a frequent contributor. She is the mother of three boys.

LOUISE KENNEDY is an arts reporter for the *Boston Globe*, where she was a longtime contributor to the Sunday magazine's "In Person" column. She is the coauthor, with Linda K. Rath, PhD, of *The Between the Lions Book for Parents* (HarperCollins, 2004).

CAROLINE LEAVITT is a book columnist for the *Boston Globe* and *Imagine* magazine, and an award-winning writer of eight novels, including *Girls in Trouble* and *Coming Back to Me*. Her writing has appeared in *Salon, Redbook, Parenting,* the *Chicago Tribune,* the *Washington Post,* and more. She lives in Hoboken, New Jersey, with her husband, the writer Jeff Tamarkin, their young son, Max, and a cranky tortoise.

KATHERINE LEE is a contributing editor at *Working Mother* magazine, a former editor at *Parenting* magazine, and is a freelance writer whose work has been published in *Parenting, Pregnancy,* and other national magazines.

MUFFY MEAD-FERRO is the bestselling author of *Confessions of a Slacker Mom* (Da Capo/Lifelong Books, 2004) and *Confessions of a Slacker Wife* (Da Capo/Lifelong Books, 2005). She lives with her husband, Michael, and two children in Salt Lake City, Utah.

JACQUELYN MITCHARD is the author of the number-one *New York Times* bestselling novel *The Deep End of the Ocean,* chosen as the first book for Oprah's Book Club, as well as the bestsellers *Twelve Times Blessed, A Theory of Relativity,* and *The Most Wanted.* She writes a nationally syndicated column, "The Rest of Us," and is a contributing editor for *Ladies' Home Journal* and *Parenting* magazine. She lives in Madison, Wisconsin, with her husband and six children.

JUDITH NEWMAN is the author of *You Make Me Feel Like an Unnatural Woman,* a memoir about becoming a mother late in life. She is a freelance writer whose work has appeared in many publications, including *Vanity Fair, National Geographic, Vogue, Ladies' Home Journal, Self*, and the *New York Times*.

ASRA Q. NOMANI is the author of the critically acclaimed *Standing Alone in Mecca: An American Woman's Struggle for the Soul of Islam*. A former *Wall Street Journal* correspondent, Nomani has also written for the *Washington Post*, the *New York Times*, and *Time* magazine on Islam. She covered the war in Afghanistan for *Salon*, and her work has appeared in *Cosmo, Sports Illustrated for Women*, and *People*. Nomani is the author of *Tantrika* (HarperSanFrancisco, 2003) and currently lives in Morgantown, West Virginia, with her son, Shibli. There, she has become a writer-activist dedicated to reclaiming women's rights and principles of tolerance in the Muslim world.

RONNIE POLANECZKY is an award-winning columnist at the *Philadelphia Daily News*. Her work has appeared in *Good House-keeping, Ladies' Home Journal, Redbook, Child, Reader's Digest,* and *Parenting*. She lives in Philadelphia with her husband and daughter.

SUSAN REIMER is a columnist for the *Baltimore Sun*, where she has worked as a writer since 1979. Her column is distributed internationally by Tribune Media and won the prestigious National Headliner Award in 2003. She is author of *Motherhood Is a Contact Sport*, and lives with her husband, sportswriter Gary Mihoces, in Annapolis, Maryland.

TEME WEINSTEIN RING lives with her family in Wilmette, Illinois. She is the editor of *Canary Times*, the quarterly support group publication of the Chronic Fatigue Syndrome, Fibromyalgia and Chemical Sensitivity Coalition of Chicago.

MARIA RODRIQUEZ is a pseudonym for a freelance writer born and raised in Mexico.

JENNY ROSENSTRACH is a special projects editor at *Real Simple*. She lives in Dobbs Ferry, New York, with her husband and two daughters.

PAMELA REDMOND SATRAN is the author of the new novel *Suburbanistas*, published by Downtown Press, as well as the novels *Younger*, *Babes in Captivity*, and *The Man I Should Have Married*. The coauthor of the bestselling baby-naming guides *Beyond Jennifer & Jason, Madison & Montana* and *Cool Names*, she is a contributing editor to *Parenting* magazine.

WENDY SCHUMAN is the managing editor of Beliefnet.com and the producer/editor of its book series, published by Rodale and Doubleday. She is also the former executive editor of *Parents* magazine. She has two grown children and lives with her husband in Cedar Grove, New Jersey.

ROCHELLE SHAPIRO is the author of the novel *Miriam the Medium* (Simon & Schuster, 2004). Her work has been published in the *New York Times*, *Newsweek*, and several literary magazines and anthologies.

HELENE STAPINSKI is the author of the bestselling memoir *Five-Finger Discount: A Crooked Family History* and *Baby Plays Around: A Love Affair, with Music*. Her work has been published in the *New York Times*, *New York* magazine, *Real Simple*, and *Salon*, among other publications. She lives in Brooklyn with her husband, son, and daughter.

KATHARINE WEBER is the author of the novels *Objects in the Mirror Are Closer Than They Appear*, *The Music Lesson*, and *The Little Women*. All three were *New York Times Book Review* Notable Books. Her fourth novel is forthcoming from Farrar, Straus and Giroux. She has taught fiction writing at Yale University, the Paris Writers Workshop, and elsewhere, and her short stories, essays, and criticism have appeared in a range of publications, among them *The New Yorker*, the *London Review of Books*, the *New York Times Book Review*, and *Vogue*. More information can be found at www.katharineweber.com.

MARY ELIZABETH WILLIAMS is the Table Talk host for *Salon*, and writes for the *New York Times*, the *New York Observer*, *TV Guide*, and other publications. She lives in Brooklyn with her husband and two daughters.